Understanding Yourself

A SPIRITUAL APPROACH
TO SELF-DISCOVERY
AND SOUL-AWARENESS

Understanding Yourself

MARK L. PROPHET
ELIZABETH CLARE PROPHET

SUMMIT UNIVERSITY PRESS®

UNDERSTANDING YOURSELF
A Spiritual Approach to Self-Discovery and Soul-Awareness
by Mark L. Prophet and Elizabeth Clare Prophet.
Copyright © 1979, 1982, 1999 by Summit University Press.
All rights reserved. Revised edition.

Library of Congress Catalog Card Number: 76-28089
ISBN: 0-916766-46-2

SUMMIT UNIVERSITY ❧ PRESS®
Summit University Press and ❧ are registered trademarks.
Printed in the United States of America
04 03 02 01 00 99   6 5 4 3 2 1

To the Seeker for the Real Self

Contents

Note: Because gender-neutral language can be cumbersome and at times confusing, we have used the pronouns *he* and *him* to refer to God or to the individual and *man* or *mankind* to refer to people in general. We have used these terms for readability and consistency, and they are not intended to exclude women or the feminine aspect of the Godhead. God is both masculine and feminine. We do, however, use the pronouns *she* and *her* to refer to the soul because each soul, whether housed in a male or female body, is the feminine counterpart of the masculine Spirit.

Man, Know Thy Self…

1

Consciousness Is the Doorway to Reality

He who has not known himself has known
nothing, but he who has known himself has at
the same time already achieved knowledge
about the depth of the All.

JESUS

Self is interwoven with consciousness, and consciousness is the doorway to reality. In an impure state, consciousness puts out the light; in a pure state, it radiates light.

The admonishment "Let your light so shine before men, that they may see your good works and glorify your Father which is in heaven"[1] is both blessing and reproof. It is a blessing to those who follow it and a reproof to those who do not. But the purpose of life is not to reprove; it is to cultivate the qualities of reality.

The appearance world is a world of illusion. Yet it seems real, and to some even the idiosyncrasies of the human personality take on a form of reality.

Our subject, understanding yourself, is a broad one. We would softly yet skillfully pull the thread of man's consciousness through the eye of the needle into the world of crystal clarity.

From the standpoint of the human mind, how sad it is that illusions must be shattered. But we deem it far wiser and less painful to shatter them by the skillful use of spiritual discernment than to have them broken by the impact of the higher law as that law brings to the doorstep of each man a return of the negative energies he has sent out.

The Yearning for Friendship with God and Man

Let us journey through the night of human reason. As we pass through the undergrowth of a wilderness land, suddenly a light appears! It is a light set upon a hill.[2] We perceive an old castle dimly through the mist. And the feeble beam from the window is a glowing filament of hope.

Someone is there—someone who will welcome us. We approach with caution. Yet as we draw near, the heart rejoices in anticipation of a warm reception. Yes, the hope the heart holds to hear the word "friend" is very great.

And so we come first to the Golden Rule, "Do unto others as you would have them do unto you."[3] Through our use and misuse of God's energy, we draw to ourselves the chain of affinities that links many of our past lives to the present one.

Sometimes the skeins of recognition appear in a momentary thread of contact. A touch long forgotten sparks a human relationship as souls contact the bitter and the sweet of passing experience. Place this motif against the light in the castle window and realize how men search the past in their longing for acceptance, for friendship, for decency and for a sense of belonging.

Spiritual and Material Unity

Ask yourself these questions: Does the eternal Creator create without the hope of spiritual unity for his creation? Should unity be only spiritual or should it be both spiritual and material?

When you are conscious of the flame of life blazing on the altar of your heart, you become aware of the supernatural as well as the natural qualities of life. Sometimes these qualities change. The natural may take on supernatural or unusual qualities whereas the supernatural may appear natural.

Regardless of what anyone may do to you, there is never an excuse for you to return in kind an act of evil. This does not preclude the possibility of the individual, in the dignity of his being, avoiding subservience to human nonsense. Therefore, out of reverence for the flame that burns on the altar of the heart, men can extend the balm of forgiveness to everyone they meet without becoming a victim of vicious energies.

It is our purpose to set forth for all who would follow in the footsteps of the ascended and unascended masters the wisdom of God that does not mock man's efforts to emulate his Creator. We convey hope and the thread of contact. We convey a sense of unity with the Brothers of the Golden Robe. But above all, we alert our students to the great need to construct nobility of character in imitation of the Divine.

Freedom from Oppressive States of Mind

Let all, then, learn the lesson of loving friend and foe alike. Sometimes friends are more dangerous than foes. For enemies are known to be enemies, but friends are known only as friends even though they may have critical and controlling thoughts that are almost audible. Sewn just beneath the surface of self-awareness, threads of selfishness often motivate people to seek unrighteous control over the lives of others.

When advice is sought, it can be offered with impunity. When advice is offered without being sought, frequently it becomes karmic responsibility. And when it is spurned, the invisible clash between minds creates karma for both parties.

Turbulence and tension between people sometimes leaves one with a sinking feeling in the belly. This is because all discord sets up an interference to the pattern of light-energy which flows through the solar plexus. The first step toward wholesome integration with the Divine Presence is to remove tension from one's four lower bodies—the physical body, the desire body, the mental body and the memory body.

As the years pass, so do lifetimes. Human affairs are often entangling. But the best way to disentangle oneself and one's energies from karmic patterns which return to us for redemption is to maintain a sense of unity with the Creator and with all of his sons and daughters. Just because you have had problems with people does not mean that those problems should continue. Let your experiences teach your soul how to find freedom from oppressive states of mind.

Anger Spells Danger to the Soul

When men mock principle and violate the sacred tenets of life, it may stir a sense of indignation within others, and rightfully so. There is such a thing as righteous anger, but this involves principle not person—such as when Jesus drove the moneychangers out of the temple.[4]

One should never direct anger toward another person. Just as a storm cloud covers the sun, so dark clouds of anger cover the sun of the soul. Therefore, we must heed the apostle's warning "Let not the sun go down upon your wrath."[5] The consequences of not heeding this warning are indeed grave.

If one goes to sleep at night harboring unrighteous anger against another, his astral sheath, known as the *ka,* may go out from him charged with that anger, targeting it at the unsuspecting victim of his wrath. Even without one's conscious awareness, the unchecked anger could be the instrument of another's misfortune or even sudden death.

While a person sleeps, the subconscious mind is in control. Ungoverned by the conscious, discriminating Christ mind, the ghostlike *ka* sets out to fulfill one's unbridled desires. When he awakens in the morning, he will have no memory of the misdeeds of his *ka.* Nevertheless, he will be karmically accountable for the harm his subconscious wreaked upon an enemy or an innocent victim.

So, ere the sun sets and you retire at night, it is

important to make your peace with God and man at all levels of consciousness.[6]

Open the Door to Joy and Reality

When men wear the garb of greed or egoism, they cloak themselves in nonsensical idiosyncrasies. When they shape their lives by whimsy rather than by the geometry of cosmic law, when they imagine God to be wholly impersonal, having no personal interest in them or their fate, they close the door to joy and reality.

In these sixteen chapters on understanding yourself, Lanto, Meru and I would open your consciousness to the doorway of reality. We come to fill the soul, the mind, the consciousness and the being of man with an awareness that will break the chains that have bound him to the limitations of his mortality.

We wish to restore the boundaries of the temple of God in man and in woman and to reassert the individual's right to take dominion over his own life. We come to guide him in his search for ultimate reality and to assure him that we are very much present in the universe as his teachers, as his brothers and as his friends. As we represent God to the evolutions of earth, so may each individual.

To one who is beginning to understand himself as a component of God, the world is a stella nova. He is refreshed in the dawn of each new day. The world is born anew all around him. His weary soul sheds its fantasies and frustrations. At last he opens his eyes to behold reality.

From the beginning to the ending of time, God has sent ministering angels to instruct his children in the ways of self-mastery which would lead them to their reunion with him. He has sought the gradual and permanent elevation of all of his children into that vision of self that reveals the wholeness of the divine man, the Real Self.

Be at peace in God.

Lovingly, I AM

Kuthumi

2

The Essence of
Higher Consciousness

The entire effort of our Soul is to become
God. This effort is as natural to man
as that of flying is to birds.

MARSILIO FICINO

The happiness one feels when
he consciously directs the flow of his energy one-point-
edly toward the goal of union with God is an expression
of universal harmony.

As people seek to commune with the essence of their
own being, they must see that God has implanted his
divine seed within them, even as he has implanted it in
nature. As fourteenth-century mystic Meister Eckhart
wrote: "There is something in the soul that is so akin to
God that it is one with Him.[1] God's seed is within us."[2]

Each seed bears after its kind. Each creature begets

its likeness. Inasmuch as God made man and woman to be free agents of himself, they should understand the meaning of freedom in their exercise of free will. That freedom is nowhere better expressed than in the seed that God has planted within us.

Third-century Church Father Origen of Alexandria wrote: "Since God Himself has sown this seed, impressed and impregnated it, it can indeed be covered over and hidden, but never destroyed or extinguished in itself; it glows and gleams, shines and burns and inclines without ceasing towards God."[3] Origen's keen observation of the seed's inclination toward God "without ceasing" revealed to him the independent nature of the God-free being that God made each of us to be.

Free Yourself from Unwanted Habit Patterns

Each man's cultivation of his consciousness is dominated by the patterns of mind and soul that are layered deep within his subconscious. It is because of these unseen influences that people say they don't understand themselves. They don't know why they do what they do. It is not possible for them to pry open the door of consciousness, to roam the corridors of memory and see each habit as it develops, and then to weed out undesirable thought patterns.

There is a better way. And that way is the saturation

of one's consciousness with the flame of cosmic worth. The word of Moses "Our God is a consuming fire"[4] is a source of great comfort to those who understand it, for the Divine One is ablaze with benevolent blessings that he pours out upon his people.

The pulsations of the sacred fire within man and woman convey in their naturalness the essence of each one's higher consciousness. These pulsations deactivate much of the malintent that may be locked within the subconscious. Within the cell structure, they create and re-create the most outstanding imprints reflective of cosmic law.

Receive these patterns from the divine source day by day and enter into the higher consciousness they convey. In time you may then free yourself from the unwanted habit patterns of the human consciousness. You will draw nigh to God even as God draws nigh to you.[5]

Invoking the Flames of God

The overshadowing of the human consciousness by the divine consciousness takes place when the devotee kneels at the altar of the heart and invokes the flames of God. The regular worship of the God-flame within the secret chamber of the heart will magnetize to the devotee the sense of his own reality as the reality of God.

Most people have experienced this in the innocence

of babyhood and early childhood. Those who would reenter such direct communion would do well to approach the sweetness of God and seek his companionship, even as he walked and talked with Adam and Eve in the garden.

Devotees of the mind of God have practiced the ritual of passing the flames of God through their consciousness for centuries. One does this by invoking each of the flames of the seven rays in succession.

The flames of God focus the energies of the seven rays of God—the First Ray, the Second Ray, and so forth. Their colors in the order of the rays are blue, yellow, pink (or rose), white, green, purple and gold, and violet.

In the ritual of the passing of the flames, one visualizes each of the rays in succession. He simultaneously calls to the divine source to direct the flames through him as powerful beams. He sees them pass through his four lower bodies, through his chakras, through his major and minor organs and bodily systems, and through the superconscious, the conscious, the subconscious and the unconscious compartments of his identity.

Through this ritual, the devotee purifies himself as a prelude to self-emptying. To self-empty is to prepare the narrow room of self-awareness for the influx of the greater God-Self awareness that one may acquire day by day incrementally through this ritual of the passing of the flames.

As you visualize the seven rays passing through you, voice a powerful fiat unto the Lord with profound gratitude and the expectation of its immediate fulfillment: "O Lord, expand my narrow room!"

Say it again and again with deep devotion. Note how you approach closer and closer to the divine source through the love you pour into the worded matrix of this fiat. Each time you give this fiat aloud in full voice, God expands the capacity of your lower self to contain the Higher Self.

With each repetition of this ritual, the devotee intensifies the action of the flames within the dimensions of his "narrow room" until one day he discovers that his narrow room now contains the vastness of his cosmic consciousness.

Universal Symptoms of Unhappiness:
The Five Poisons

Each chapter we unfold focuses on one of the universal diseases of unhappiness. The sincere seeker for truth will receive maximum benefit from this course if he will create a mental road map that will guide him to the correct understanding of the self through his pursuit of the teachings of the ascended masters.

It would also be helpful for him to outline tried and true methods of overcoming bad habits and undesirable qualities that he has appended to the self. By so doing, he can alleviate and even entirely eliminate the symptoms of unhappiness which Tibetan Buddhists call the "five poisons."

The five poisons are antidoted by the five wisdoms of the Five Dhyani Buddhas and Vajrasattva. The Dhyani Buddhas are celestial Buddhas. The Tibetan Buddhists believe that the Adi-Buddha, the primordial highest being, created the Dhyani Buddhas by his meditative powers.

The Five Dhyani Buddhas and Vajrasattva are considered to be great healers of the mind and soul. They are not historical figures, like Gautama Buddha, but transcendent beings who symbolize universal divine principles or forces. They represent various aspects of the enlightened consciousness and are guides to spiritual transformation.

How to Eliminate the Five Poisons

The Tibetan Book of the Dead recommends that the devotee meditate on the Dhyani Buddhas so that their wisdoms will replace the negative forces he has allowed to take hold within.

Vairochana's all-pervading wisdom of the Dharmakaya (the God Presence) antidotes the poison of ignorance.

Akshobhya's mirrorlike wisdom antidotes the poison of anger and hatred.

Ratnasambhava's wisdom of equality antidotes the poison of spiritual, intellectual and human pride.

Amitabha's discriminating wisdom antidotes the poison of the passions—all cravings, covetousness, greed and lust.

Amoghasiddhi's all-accomplishing wisdom, the wisdom of perfected action, antidotes the poison of envy and jealousy.

Vajrasattva's wisdom of the diamond will of God antidotes the poisons of non-will and non-being, fear, doubt and non-belief in God.

Each Dhyani Buddha has a *bija,* or seed syllable, that represents his essence. It can be used along with the sacred syllable *Om* and the Buddha's name to create a mantra (a series of mystic syllables that have an esoteric meaning).

You can repeat the following mantras to the Dhyani Buddhas to align yourself with the divine qualities they represent and receive the blessing of their transcendent powers.

Om Vairochana Om
Om Akshobhya Hum
Om Ratnasambhava Tram
Om Amitabha Hrih

Om Amoghasiddhi Ah
Om Vajrasattva Hum

You Can Return to Innocence

The soul who earnestly seeks the knowledge of self must return to that state of innocence which has no need to defend itself against a host of enemies. It is not that we would deactivate those defenses that are certainly necessary to the protection of one's spiritual life, one's family or one's livelihood.

Nevertheless, we ask you to set them aside temporarily during your study of our teachings so that your consciousness might once again enter the happy state it knew before its mechanisms were warped by the verdicts of men. Samuel Taylor Coleridge spoke of this happy state as "that willing suspension of disbelief for the moment, which constitutes poetic faith."[6]

Why have people hardened their hearts toward one another and their God? Our answer in part is that they have been on both the giving and receiving ends of this self-destructive state of being.

Karma Dodging

It is written that the LORD prophesied that he would harden Pharaoh's heart, and he did. And Pharaoh in his pride hardened his own heart toward Moses and the children of Israel. In this instance, the LORD heaped upon Pharaoh what Pharaoh had heaped upon God's chosen people. God let Pharaoh's karma fall and Pharaoh in turn tried to unload it on the children of Israel.

Pharaoh's reaction to his return of karma is called karma dodging. But in this case, it soon backfired. God parted the Red Sea, the Israelites crossed over, Pharaoh's chariots and his hosts followed in their wake and were engulfed in the sea as it closed around them.

Again we ask, why do some people harden their hearts? For them it is the law of the circle: What others have "dished out" to them, they in turn "dish out" to others.

Not all understand that the true law of the circle is the law of karma and that they can rise above the limitations of their karma. Yet some, without knowing this law, have embraced it in their fastidious practice of the Golden Rule. They do unto others as they would have others do unto them.

They forgive seventy times seven, walking the extra mile, blessing those that curse them, doing good to those that hate them, praying for those who despitefully use them and persecute them, judging not that they be not judged, and so forth.

Those who are harsh in word and deed will surely find that the law of the circle will one day carry their harshness back to their own doorstep. And when it does, they are often the ones who are first to chafe at the bit of their own karma as it returns for resolution and redemption. As the villainous Edmund says in Shakespeare's *King Lear* when affairs turn against him and he is mortally wounded by his half brother, Edgar, "The wheel is come full circle."[7]

Taking Accountability for Your Actions

Often people who have not been taught the law of the circle, or the law of karma, do not take accountability for their actions, much less for their thoughts and feelings. They want someone else to pay the price. They seek a vicarious atonement.

They say: "Jesus died for my sins. He paid the price. I have accepted him as my Saviour. He has atoned for me. I am free of all accountability now and forever."

This is a misunderstanding of Jesus' teachings. In his Sermon on the Mount, Jesus teaches the consequences of doing good and doing evil. He places squarely on the shoulders of the individual his responsibility to obey the laws of God and man—else he will pay the uttermost farthing.

Some people want to be free of all responsibility. They deem it their right to damage others—physically, emotionally, mentally and spiritually. Because of their hardness of heart and their insensitivity to life, they do not allow themselves to get in touch and stay in touch with their own feelings. Hence they do not respond to others with feelings of compassion and understanding but only with hate and more hate.

Yet all of this began early in this life or in a number of past lives. The past-life equation in this dilemma makes it difficult for people to get to the core of self to finally discover the root cause of their immense karmic burden.

In the meantime, they are capable of expressing great dislike for the qualities of mercy, justice, compassion, kindness—and especially forgiveness—which in moments of stress they expect others to heap upon them. What they think to accomplish by stressing their own importance through destroying the self-respect of others remains a mystery to many.

Walk the Earth in Dignity

By contrast, the great teachers of mankind have walked the earth showing men how to live by dispensing both practical and spiritual wisdom. Their instructions have been simple. They have taught men not to hate but to love. Their admonishments were codified in the Ten Commandments and in the founding principles of the world's major religions.

These principles include a belief in one Supreme

Being, who may become manifest to man through avatars or great spiritual teachers; a recognition that man reaps what he sows; an injunction to truth, honesty, justice and other social virtues; and an entreaty to remain humble before God, as well as before God in man.

For the most part, these precepts were accepted by those who heard them. Yet when the first tests of the Law and the Lawgiver came upon them, they reacted as though they had never been schooled in the righteousness of God. Stung with self-righteous indignation before the banal acts of barbaric souls, they abandoned both the disciplines and the compassion of the Law and the Lawgiver and descended to a primitive approach to problem solving. They hurled clubs and curses and murdered and maimed without remorse.

The reactions of modern man to his pent-up anger against God and society are not far from the ancient responses of his primitive forebears. But today, through the teachings of the ascended masters, each one can walk the earth in dignity overshadowed by his God Presence. Each one can embrace the gift of love, both giving and receiving that special gift of charity that is meet for all. Yes, all can espouse the Be-attitude of affirming God's Be-ness in one another.

Seek to Replicate Heavenly Patterns

Attitude is all-important. It is like a sieve through which the pulp of life is pressed. Verily, what comes out is molded by one's attitude. What comes out is one's life essence that one may then choose to pour into matrices of right mindfulness or wrong mindfulness.

It is essential that every follower of truth recognize the folly of patterning his life after self-limiting human paradigms. Instead he must enter the grid of the great patterns of the Law that undergird the universe. And he must know that these patterns also exist within himself.

Yes, man the microcosm contains the grid of the macrocosm. He must pattern his life after the patterns made perfect in the heavens and seek to replicate them in the earth and in his four lower bodies. For in these perfect patterns he shall find the peace that passes the understanding of the human archetype in favor of the divine.

This peace comes when he kisses the hands and the feet of the law of God as his saviour. For this law is indeed his saviour when it leads him to the path of eternal life. Likewise is this law his saviour when it frees his mind from the dregs of darkness that have taken hold of it.

You Are a Spiritual-Material Being

We dare not eliminate the tares from the field of human consciousness without taking into account that if we do so prematurely we may also uproot the good wheat.[8] It is known that when the shoots are young the tares and the wheat look alike. And so they are left to grow side by side until the harvest. When they are mature and ready to harvest, they are easily separated. The tares are gathered and bound in bundles to be burned, and the wheat is gathered into the barn.

The safest way to eliminate the tares of the human consciousness before they choke the wheat of the divine consciousness is to use the flames of God. But men seldom realize just what the flames are, and when we speak of them they are often puzzled.[9]

Let us repeat, then, that there is a natural order and universe, and there is a spiritual order and universe. The glory of the terrestrial is one and the glory of the celestial is another.[10] The flames of God are of the spiritual order; and these, by the grace of God, penetrate the natural order with the transforming power of the Holy Spirit.[11]

The experiences of the devotee who loves truth enough to search it out will help him understand that the qualities of God are inherent within the spiritual order. Although these qualities penetrate the material order, they do not originate in it. It is, therefore, in the correct understanding of matter in its relationship to Spirit that men become enlightened.

To understand oneself as a spiritual-material being is to apprehend one's relationship to others. To understand the need to purify one's consciousness (insofar as it has taken on a limited, self-centered view or existence) is to apprehend one's relationship to life as a whole.

The reception of God's consciousness as though one's physical form, one's mind and one's self-awareness were wholly permeated with the energy of creation will produce in one's total being the godly estate that is desired. When you cultivate this estate, you will be fortified to cast out the mind's negative proclivities. In their place you will come to know the joy, the hope and the love of the infinite mind of God as it descends into your finite world.

Cast Out the Enemy Within

Your Christ mind is your armour against the insidious forces that lurk within the subconscious and the unconscious levels of being. Another term for these levels is the *electronic belt*. This belt extends from the waist to beneath the feet. It is shaped like a large kettledrum. It contains the aggregate records of your negative thoughts, feelings, words and deeds, hence your negative karma.

When man contacts the vital flames of the Creator's consciousness, he transports himself out of the confines of his mortality into the spiritual realms of his immortality. The soul's deep desire to be transported out of the realm of the ordinary into the realm of the extraordinary is tantamount to offering a fervent prayer to God for her self-transformation. But when she also expresses a willingness to be decontaminated from all undesirable qualities, she opens the floodgates of her mind to the light of God, which then rushes into the compartments of her being to expurgate all negative vibrations.

Beneath the surface calm are caverns of consciousness which may be in a state of turmoil. This is often indicative of a polarization of negative karma within the psyche. This karma, spawned in near and distant epochs of personal history, is the underlying cause of schism within the self.

To cast out the enemy within by invoking the sacred fire is a necessary process. When you do this, transmutation takes place and the energies that you have imprisoned in matrices of imperfect thought and feeling are released.

Your Causal Body Records All Positive Karma

Immediately after having been dislodged from the electronic belt and purified by the flames of God, these energies ascend to your Causal Body. This is the body of first cause and it is the repository of all God-good that you have ever externalized.

Just as the electronic belt bears the record and the misqualified substance of negative human karma, so the Causal Body bears the burden of light that records all positive karma. The Causal Body, then, is of the spiritual order and universe, and the four lower bodies and the electronic belt are of the natural order and universe.

The glory of the celestial body is the means whereby we overcome and transcend the terrestrial body. In the words of Saint Paul:

> [The terrestrial body] is sown in corruption; it is raised in incorruption.
>
> It is sown in dishonor; it is raised in glory. It is sown in weakness; it is raised in power.
>
> It is sown a natural body; it is raised a spiritual body. There is a natural body, and there is a spiritual body.
>
> And so it is written, The first man Adam was made a living soul; the last Adam was made a quickening spirit.[12]

The tenderness of the Divine One is a boon of great comfort to all who trust in the LORD with all their hearts and lean not to their own understanding.[13] When you invest your faith in the living God, he will multiply that faith and return to you untold blessings.

It is well to remember the words from Hebrews: "Faith is the substance of things hoped for, the evidence of things not seen."[14] When you are childlike in your faith, that faith will sustain you in your determination to find your freedom from the darkness that would hide your True Self.

May wisdom lead you to the Light and the Light to God's happiness.

Victoriously, I remain

Lanto

3

The Art of Self-Discovery

God said to Abram, "Go to your self,
know your self, fulfill your self."

THE ZOHAR

The quest for self-discovery is sparked by the still small voice of God that can be heard in the precincts of the heart, spurring the soul to discover the mysteries of creation. But this voice is often ignored when man is snarled in the minutiae of karmic interaction. The human intellect inevitably falls into the trap of overconcern about the details of life.

All might take a lesson from a conversation overheard between a robin and a sparrow:

> Said the Robin to the Sparrow:
> "I should really like to know
> Why these anxious human beings
> Rush about and worry so."

Said the Sparrow to the Robin:
"Friend, I think that it must be
That they have no heavenly Father
Such as cares for you and me."[1]

One foolproof method of escape from self-centeredness can be found in the principle of nonattachment to the fruit of action as espoused by the Buddhas and Bodhisattvas. This principle was also taught by the Master Jesus Christ when he said, "He that findeth his life shall lose it: and he that loseth his life for my sake shall find it."[2]

Let us pause for a moment to be certain we understand the profound meaning of this saying, for it is pivotal in the understanding of one's personal psychology. When a person finds his life, he inevitably becomes attached to his life. But it is this very attachment which sets in motion the forces that will eventually cause him to lose his life. I would explain to my students this universal law.

Overcome Idolatry and Gain Eternal Life

God's first commandment given to Moses says, "Thou shalt have no other gods before me."[3] If we make a god of ourselves and our lifestyle, we are both self-idolatrous and self-attached.

And by and by, the Great Lawgiver will take from us the life we have become attached to. For he has said, "I, the LORD thy God, am a jealous God, visiting the iniquity of the fathers upon the children unto the third and fourth generation of them that hate me and showing mercy unto thousands of them that love me and keep my commandments."[4]

God is our Divine Lover. He says: "I want all of you. Nothing less will suffice. If you give all of yourself to me, I will give all of myself to you. But if you cleave unto your separate self—that part of yourself that has separated out from me—and you set yourself up as a god in your own right, then it shall be written in your book of life that you have placed the god of yourself before me and thereby entered into self-idolatry. Thus your karma shall be upon you, and your days in the earth shall be numbered.

"Furthermore, because you have not cleaved unto me, I will take from you the God-identification that I have given you. For I have endowed you with a selfhood that is made in the image and likeness of my Selfhood.

"Therefore, if you desire to make your being permanent in my Being, you must surrender your lesser self unto my Greater Self. In so doing, you shall gain eternal life. Thus, he who loses his life for my sake shall indeed find it again."

Selfless Service Leads to Ultimate Freedom

It is difficult for people who have not contributed selflessly to the well-being of others to give up their day-to-day sense that life is a struggle. The ascended master Saint Germain once said, "It is ever a sense of struggle which makes the struggle." If you really want to vanquish the sense of struggle, we would recommend that you systematically engage in selfless service to others. For by and by, the kindness you give will open the door to a spiritual path of joyous self-discovery.

The danger attendant upon your supposed selfless service is that it may not be selfless at all but offered that all men may think well of you. The rabbi Jesus Christ admonished those who professed to be engaged in selfless service but did so publicly for all to see:

> Take heed that ye do not your alms before men, to be seen of them: otherwise ye have no reward of your Father which is in heaven.
>
> Therefore when thou doest thine alms, do not sound a trumpet before thee, as the hypocrites do in the synagogues and in the streets, that they may have glory of men. Verily I say unto you, They have their reward.
>
> But when thou doest alms, let not thy left hand know what thy right hand doeth:

That thine alms may be in secret: and thy Father which seeth in secret himself shall reward thee openly.[5]

The key to freedom is to serve and search. Let your service be constant and let your search not be a forced penetration of the mysteries of life but a gentle expectancy that promotes discovery.

The Analytical Mind Strips the Soul Naked

One of the road blocks you may encounter as you seek to discover your Real Self is the human tendency to analyze yourself and others. The analytical mind strips the soul naked even as it destroys its fabric. So delicate is this fabric that you must leave it untouched and protect it from the hand of human reason. Analyzing the human self without taking into consideration the divine component of the Higher Self is a scorched-earth approach that kills both the tares and the wheat[6] and leaves the naked soul comfortless.

In a similar vein, those who attempt to "deprogram" people from their religious beliefs violently tear from them not only the ideas that the deprogrammers consider harmful but also the very fabric of the soul's contact with God. It is as though their minds were scraped with oyster shells. And many who have gone through deprogramming never have their faith restored in this life.

Jesus taught that "from the days of John the Baptist until now, the kingdom of heaven suffereth violence and the violent take it by force."[7] This violence was a direct assault against the kingdom of God manifest in the persons of John the Baptist and Jesus Christ, and it is also directed against souls today.

Sometimes in therapy the mind suffers the violence of analysis through an insensitive therapist. This can prove harmful to the unsuspecting soul. It is analogous to the soldiers of Pontius Pilate stripping Jesus of his garments before nailing him to the cross.

Those who analyze the mind, the heart, the soul and the spirit of others without helping to erect the pillars of God's consciousness in their temple do a disservice to all. This sort of compartmentalized view of personhood does not account for the threefold flame as the God-center of identity, verily the Deity within.

The Kingdom of God
Is the Consciousness of God

The inner meaning of the word *kingdom* is "consciousness." Both John and Jesus embodied the kingdom, as the consciousness, of God. In those days, some were not willing to subject themselves to John and Jesus, that they might study to show themselves approved unto God, workmen that needeth not to be ashamed, rightly dividing the word of truth.[8] They were too proud to enter in by the strait gate, to pass their tests day by day until the great Law itself should bestow upon each one the divine approbation: "Well done, thou good and faithful servant. Thou hast been faithful over a few things; I will make thee ruler over many things. Enter thou into the joy of thy lord."[9]

John and Jesus suffered violence against their persons. As a result of their witness, many resolved to become their disciples. These were resolutely determined to press on and to enter into the kingdom, the consciousness, of God.

And so, let our students quicken their resolve to lawfully enter into the inner sanctum of being. We recommend that through soulful prayer and deep meditation, you develop a sense of sweet surrender to cosmic purpose as it pertains to you, even though that purpose be unknown to you.

Faith in the Universality of God

The greatest masters, both ascended and unascended, have ultimately obtained reality through their abiding faith in the constancy of cosmic law. Not one has ever obtained reality through the intellect alone or by probing the caverns of the subconscious mind. Furthermore, they have proven that one cannot discover good by probing evil.

Only by faith in the universality of the Fatherhood of God—and a sense of being nurtured by the Motherhood of God—can one approach divine Sonship through the life-giving energies of the Universal Christ. And thereby the soul is nourished with the milk, and by and by the meat, of the living Word.

To a greater or lesser extent, mankind have ignored the divine mandates that have been handed down to them by the great Manus, or lawgivers, who sponsored the world's races and religions. What a pity! For to ignore the guidelines of the sacred scriptures of East and West leaves one with the dry leaves of secularism, sophistry and a science without God.

Where there is no God, man elevates himself to the throne of deity. Thus many man-made gods roam the earth. This approach is destructive to the soul and her godward aspirations.

Reality Shuns Dualism

The highest truth man can discover is reality. For when he knows he is real, having touched the hem of reality's garment, he leaves behind the testimony of the human senses. In reality there is no need to qualify the moment-by-moment reportings of the five senses. He has but to enter the realm of the spiritual senses to know himself as being ultimately real.

This reality shuns dualism. For only God is real, and God and man are one, not two. Man knows himself as the extension of God on earth, his hands and feet. He is of God, and God is both with him and in him. Therefore he, the created, is not alone but forever one with his Creator, the Uncreated One.

Unfettered by dualistic thinking and feeling, man surrenders utterly to a spiritual escalation of consciousness so vast that he merges with the very core of reality in the Great Central Sun. Ultimately, God is exalted in man and man is exalted in God. This is the ultimate reality.

God teaches man in an instant more than he could learn in thousands of years of raking over the ruins of a sunken continent or a buried civilization. God is the Creator and he tutors man when man becomes a disciple in the way of his creative culture.

Man needs to know what to do and how to do it. If he would know the what and the how of his existence, he must enter into a living relationship with the very God of his being. This relationship is forged through unadulterated devotion to the God Presence.

Without such devotion, man will never be able to convey higher teachings to another. He will be unable, whether by the spoken or written word, to show others how the soul can increase in the stature and wisdom of God. He will fail to show the soul how she might fashion her own wings that will take her soaring sunward.

The Holy Spirit Would Tutor You

We are concerned with man's evolution and specifically with his absorption, or lack thereof, of his God-given intelligence. Let those who would accelerate their learning and their learning techniques know that their devoted tutor in this vast field is the Maha Chohan, the representative of the Holy Spirit.

His retreat over Sri Lanka in the etheric octave (the heaven-world) is bristling with intense activity. Ascended and unascended devotees work feverishly, you might say, as they look forward to releasing advanced learning methods through man's higher consciousness.

Angel instructors are preparing to work with eager souls through each one's Holy Christ Self. For these instructors would teach them how to tap the infinite intelligence of the mind of God. They would teach them how to tap the storehouse of memory locked in the Causal Body as well as the momentums of man's achievements of past incarnations. These treasures, unique to every lifestream, will one day be accessed with keys held in the hand of the Holy Christ Self.

True Education Is Self-Discovery

In our sponsorship of the true education of the spirit and its application to modern teaching methods, we have no intention of belittling the educational systems of the world or the avant-garde in the field of higher education. Our goal is to convey secular and spiritual knowledge to humanity that will allow them to appreciate the art of self-discovery. But when the system becomes an end in itself, rather than a means to an end, we become concerned.

The macrocosm of God mirrors in the microcosm of man the reality of the self in its highest state. When one is made aware of the reflection of God that is within himself, he is changed in a moment—in the twinkling of an eye. He finds his reason for being.

He must project the image and likeness of God upon his own soul and inner vision, that the patterns in the heavens may be reflected in the earth through him. Then he must project the image and likeness of God upon all whom he meets.

He sees the multiplication of the God Presence one by one by one over every living soul. Yet he comprehends the law of the One: "Hear, O Israel, the LORD our God is one LORD."[10] He sees the oversoul and understands that the one God personalizes himself in every one of his sons and daughters.

In profound humility he kneels before the unfed flame that God has placed on the altar of each one's heart. He discovers that his immortality is God's gift to him. He vows that he will love, honor and obey the God within until he is subsumed by him in the ritual of his soul's ascent to God, nevermore to go out. He reflects upon the mystery of his all-oneness in God and he knows that he stands always on the brink of a still greater discovery. This is self-transcendence as God wills it.

Where today can the sincere student of truth make contact with the ascended masters and their teachings? How can they make contact with the ascended master Jesus Christ, or Lao Tzu, Zarathustra or Gautama Buddha, that they might be instructed as their disciples were instructed? Who will impart to them the mysteries that these masters secretly imparted to their disciples?

Just because some have waited lifetimes to contact the teachers of truth and to sit at their feet does not mean that you should not get started. Your involvement in the business of self-discovery is the greatest assurance you can have of obtaining a passport to reality and of establishing direct contact with the ascended masters.

The Treasure of True Being

Man must build on the rock of reality. And that rock is the Universal Christ. It seems that mankind have roamed through the mists of forever, crisscrossing the land masses of earth. These have risen and fallen, shaping and reshaping a planet for Homo sapiens. And this evolution has also risen and fallen in civilizations that reached the scientific advancements of the lost continents of Atlantis and Lemuria.

But for all the glory and the infamy, the heights and the depths of mankind's shinnying up and down the DNA chain, the density and the depravity of today's extremely materialistic civilization illustrates that mankind are no closer to God than they were in prehistoric times. Through the centuries, the mores have evolved up and down and sideways, while the lusts of the flesh have robbed the sons and daughters of God of their immortal birthright.

Every child of God's heart must discover who he is. To do so, he must know his intrinsic worth. He must assess the importance he places on his spiritual path and his relationship with God, with the Holy Spirit and with the Son of God within his heart. And he must recognize his personal accomplishments—his mental grasp, his physical strength, his virtues and values, his talents and achievements.

These bright filaments of selfhood conduct the electrical currents of the I AM Presence to all who are ready to receive them. They are as stained glass windows through which the prismed light of reality can shine.

And when it shines, it carries the power of transmutation into the mind, the heart, the soul and the spirit of everyone it touches. It exposes the hidden recesses of being. It smoothens the anomalies of life. It leads the soul of light to connect with the fraternity of light. It shows her a new sense of right mindfulness. It purifies, rectifies and exalts her consciousness. It becomes the delight of her universe, the acme of her joy; for it is the jubilation of the gods.

This light is the deluxe contact with reality which will detoxify one's being of old poisons and, beyond the moment of cleansing, fill him with eternal treasure—the treasure of his true being.

The Boon of Understanding Yourself

The Darjeeling Council has selected Kuthumi, Lanto and me to tutor you in the art of self-discovery. We state at the outset that our course is a revelation from God and his ascended sons and daughters. In order to reap the greatest benefits from it, you must study it in depth and absorb it on many planes of consciousness.

The Great White Brotherhood has long desired to assist key individuals to know themselves in the context of a higher reality than they are consciously aware of. These are ripe souls, ripe for precisely this course.

We will cover many angles of the great Law from the simple to the complex. We will provide insight and new approaches to the age-old conundrums of life and death, the here and the hereafter, so that every hungry heart can be filled with the manna of spiritual understanding.

Never before in the history of planet earth have the dark ones carried an age to the brink of such massive destruction as they have contemplated and as they are capable of in this century. Yet never before have the sons and daughters of God had so much inward delight in the law of God, with its buoyant possibilities that can magnetize that indomitable will-to-be that makes of mortals immortal adepts.

Access the Light of the Universal Christ

Once again the earth must be trodden upon by embodied Gods. This is no desecration; it is the fulfillment of God's dream for every one of his sons and daughters.

Valiant souls who have the courage to be their Real Self and to consecrate that self on the altar of God will come to the fore and assume their lawful roles of leadership in all fields. They will have the vision as well as the necessary backing of the Great White Brotherhood. They will establish a universal brotherhood and sisterhood that shall recognize all people as brothers and sisters, children of the one Father-Mother God.

They will understand themselves and therefore be wise as serpents and harmless as doves. They can and shall penetrate the insidious plots of fallen angels and aliens who, if they could, would defraud the earth and its people of the solar power—that is, the "soul power" —of God's reality.

"We have seen his star in the east."[11] It is the star of the Universal Christ consciousness that can be accessed and appropriated by all servants of God worlds without end. The light from within that star must go forth, and it must reveal that which has been hidden from mankind simply because they have not been ready to receive it. The light from within that star must dispel the darkness of the long night of humanity's self-imposed suffering.

Yes, cherished reader, the light from within that star shall banish the darkness forever. There shall be no more night nor benighted understanding but only the eternal day. Therein, the elect and chosen of God shall shine in the firmament of God's universal being.

Fear not, little children; for it is your Father's good pleasure to give you the kingdom.[12] And when the Universal Christ shall appear, we shall be like him; for we shall see him as he is.[13]

In most profound peace, I AM

Meru

4

"Man, Know Thyself"

Your own Self-Realization
is the greatest service
you can render the world.

SRI RAMANA MAHARSHI

A little child is born. His life begins in hope and cherishment. Of what is he composed? Ideas? Whose ideas? God's? His parents'? His own? The world's?

Out of a panoply of ideas from heaven and earth, the soul is cloaked with her coat of many colors. And personhood steps onto life's stage.

> What is man, that thou art mindful of him? and the son of man, that thou visitest him?
>
> For thou hast made him a little lower than the angels and hast crowned him with glory and honor.

Thou madest him to have dominion over the works of thy hands; thou hast put all things under his feet:

All sheep and oxen, yea, and the beasts of the field;

The fowl of the air and the fish of the sea and whatsoever passeth through the paths of the seas.

O LORD, our LORD, how excellent is thy name in all the earth![1]

Man has many overlords, yet the God of very gods has thundered, "Thou shalt have no other gods before me!"[2] Man's gods are the rulers of the deep that are alive and well in his unconscious mind. They play hide-and-seek with him as he mirrors them, thinking they are himself even as he sees himself as a demigod. Man has allowed this intrusion into his psyche and now he must disallow it. He must clean house else he will be forcefully cleaned out of his house by his gods.

In sum, man is the slave of each of his gods. They have set up housekeeping in his being and through familiarity he has become a willing prisoner within his own four walls. Indeed, the influence of man's gods is both subtle and obvious. For example, when the karmic record is not benign it becomes an opposing force, a threatening god that must be reckoned with. Man sows; he must also reap.[3]

Learn to Manage Your Karma

The Lords of Karma seek for mankind the best resolution out of each karma-leveling experience. Yet sometimes, and seemingly without purpose, the hammer blows of so-called fate (which are actually the outcroppings of cosmic law in operation) do bring to a very low estate souls who long to rise. The cry of "Why?" is heard, but what is needed is an objective view of the self.

The seeker after his own reality must behold at a distance the outer self as well as the soul so that he may be objective in analyzing the drama of his existence. He must not permit his negative karma to be his overlord. He must learn to manage his karma through understanding himself.

Obviously karma is there. It is *the* major factor that determines the course of one's life. He cannot maneuver to the right or the left of it or pass over or under it—no, not entirely. He can dodge his karma temporarily but for just so long. Ultimately, the cudgel of the Law will catch up with him and he will pay to the last farthing, for man has created his karma and only he can uncreate it.

Returning to the subject of the karmic god in its

negative aspects, we would point out that what one cannot change one must learn to live with. And it must be remembered that the intervention of divine mercy, when the Mother of Mercy is invoked, is always a possibility for the soul who would truly serve the cause of her own freedom. In so doing, she can emerge from the entanglements of her karma.

God is always ready and willing to help. Jesus' poignant words to Saul of Tarsus "It is hard for thee to kick against the pricks"[4] reveal that when living truth first manifests itself within the domain of the human consciousness, its precepts may seem hard and its way difficult.

Rule Yourself

Now we would speak of the buildup within the self of a resistance to opposing forces both within society and in the world of the individual. We would also speak of man's desire to control others, of his desire to dominate those closest to him and of his will to rule those who would not be ruled by him. We remind you that there are gods many and lords many,[5] but the man who would truly understand himself must be subject to none of these.

Man is born to rule, but first he must rule himself. As the author of Proverbs wrote: "He that is slow to anger is better than the mighty; and he that ruleth his spirit than he that taketh a city."[6]

Man must school his desires and flex the muscles of self-control. If he cannot do this by pulling himself up by his own bootstraps, he has the right to seek divine intercession. Man is not alone. He is a unity in a diversity which in turn is held within an even greater unity.

It is just as true that all of the negative forces of the universe seem to oppose the life of the Divine Manchild aborning in the womb of the Divine Mother. It is as though the Herods of the world were sending out soldiers to slaughter the holy innocents emerging from the dense domain of personhood.

The soul must not permit herself to be overcome by her struggles against her karma. Nor should she allow herself to become embittered and to be driven into the wilderness of self-absorption.

The soul, seized with pangs of inferiority, seeks to flagellate herself and the world. She lashes out at her perceived enemies (who are really her karmic overlords, the opponents of her very existence), and in vain she tries to overcome them in an earthly way.

We are also reminded of the words of Ecclesiastes: "I have seen all the works that are done under the sun and, behold, all is vanity and vexation of spirit. That which is crooked cannot be made straight, and that which is wanting cannot be numbered."[7] But such futility and such vanity are not the purpose of life. Man must truly know himself—not as a karmic record but as a divine being.

Dethrone the God of Opposition

We come, then, to the god of the underworld who is known to all servants of truth as the god of opposition. The world seems to contain within itself the very seeds of opposition to the achievement of any good thing.

All who rise godward are opposed, and we sometimes ask ourselves if the god of opposition itself is not the goad that engenders the strength by which man achieves his goal. And if the idol be rough-hewn, then use it as a foothold for the climb.

In light of this, we remember that man must not allow himself to become subject to an overwhelming fear of the god of opposition of this world. Man must dethrone the towering gods of the underworld, not by human reason but by *holy* reason and by a purified intelligence that is one with the mind of God.

Shun the Desire to Control Others

And what of the desire to dominate others? You must recognize this desire to be one of the most dangerous diseases of the human ego—and shun it.

Only by the wings of true selfhood can you actually attain God's desire for you. And when you do, you will become a power of good example in the universe that all may follow.

As the Master Jesus so lovingly said, "Verily, verily, I say unto you, He that believeth on me, the works that I do shall he do also; and greater works than these shall he do, because I go unto my Father."[8]

As the soul rises to the level of her Holy Christ Self and then to the level of her I AM Presence, she becomes a luminary, lighting the way that others might follow the star of Christ's appearing within themselves. She opens their eyes that they may see his star, be his star, ingest his light, be possessed by his light, become his light, exalt Christ and be exalted in him. In order for the ascending soul to be such a facilitator, she must be possessed of her God-control, which mobilizes the good in all life and leads her companions on the straight and narrow way of self-mastery.

Discover and Exalt the God Within

How man trembles on the brink of self-destruction. Indeed, how he trembles on the brink of self-exaltation! Man must choose daily whether to self-destruct or to self-exalt and whether to destruct or to exalt the God within.

One way or the other, it is the outer self that trembles and not the God within. The apostle James said, "The devils also believe and tremble."[9] Yet man is not a devil (*devil* being defined as "*de*ified *evil*"). He was made a little lower than the angels and when he is found to be an overcomer, he shall be crowned with more glory and honor than God bestowed upon the angels.[10]

The little children of God must learn to fear not, for the steps to universal attainment unfold naturally within the domain of the inner self. Therefore, it is time that man discovered his inner self. If a man loses his life for the sake of his service in Christ, he shall find it again[11] in his service to Christ. This is eternal truth which cannot be gainsaid.

Man is not the little person that he seems to be. He is the great person (the pure son) that God made him to be. But he must remove the overlay of the dust and degradation of the human consciousness with the cleansing power of the Holy Spirit's sacred fire, the violet flame, and by the washing of the water by the living Word[12] that restores all things to reality. Then upon the altar stone of the inner self, he must rebuild the citadel of perfection that once stood upon the foundation of that sacred stone.

In his search for the real within himself, man can

also explore the unreal within himself. But if he merely understands what is not real, he will not of necessity bring himself to a sense of what is real. God seems far away to some, but when they draw nigh to him and he does draw nigh to them, the comfort of the Holy Spirit floods the soul with the joy of self-discovery.

God's Reality Is Your Identity

Religion has been dangled before the people as a panacea for all their ills. Formal religion is not the answer. But the reality of God, who originally clothed man with innocence, is the answer.

This purity is the fount of man's identity. Therefore, Paul wrote to the Colossians, "Lie not one to another, seeing that ye have put off the old man with his deeds and have put on the new man, which is renewed in knowledge after the image of him that created him."[13]

Discovering the reality of the God who dwells within his creation is not a matter of sect or philosophy; it is more than that. It is the living actualization of truth and of being that refuses to accept the mold of complacency, of degeneracy, of death. God's reality is the inner self that recognizes that death is the last enemy that shall be overcome,[14] together with all the lesser enemies that seek to devour personhood bite by bite.

Enemies of the Real Self

The false senses of reality must go. Not only must the soul recognize them for what they are—the enemies of the Real Self—but she must overcome them. These enemies reflect both the external and the internal life of the soul. They lie in wait to tempt the soul to waste away her substance in riotous living. Furthermore, like termites they bore into the very fabric of her being to devour her life essence.

The outer self draws discord to itself because it has already dethroned reason. Pitiful creature that he is, man does his time in the prison house of earth in the cell of his karma, ignorant of his great commission. But should he elect by free will to return to the citadel of divine reason as he begins the process of rediscovering both his outer self and his inner self, much of his sense of struggle will disappear. He will see experience as the turning of the pages in a great book on which are written not only the true senses of reality but the entire known reality of the physical universe, including the intricacies of his own soul.

Rise he must. But the answers to questions of how, why, when and where are not forthcoming to his satisfaction. The great universal magnet draws out the soul that is marking time within the shroud of the human personality.

The soul hungers to experience the true sense of reality that she knows exists somewhere. Her subtle belief in reality reflected in the majesty of the God within promises that there will be bright and better tomorrows and, above all, the option for eternal life.

Truly the admonishment "Man, know thyself!"[15] leads him upward and onward into the unfailing light.

Radiantly, I AM your elder brother,

Kuthumi

5

Identification with the Real Self

Do not go to the garden of flowers!
O Friend! go not there; In your body is the
garden of flowers. Take your seat on the
thousand petals of the lotus, and there
gaze on the Infinite Beauty.

KABIR

Anyone can answer the question "Which came first, the chicken or the egg?" Or can one? Perhaps one should pause before answering such a seemingly obvious question.

Indeed, which did come first, Creator or creation? Spirit or matter? God or man? The chicken or the egg?

Reflect for a moment on what your answer would be. For it may lead you to ponder the deeper mysteries of life as you gather layer upon layer of insight into our subject—understanding yourself.

When God created man and woman to be spiritual beings, living spirits molded out of his eternal spirit yet encased in bodies of clay, he fully endowed them with the faculties of his universal consciousness. Now, universal consciousness may be defined as God's universal awareness of himself. However, God's universal self-awareness functions not only within the domain of spirit but also within the time-space continuum of the material universe.

Because man is both godlike and manlike, he is able to integrate his higher and lower personalities, both the spiritual and the material. And it is his responsibility to do so. It is also his responsibility to integrate within himself the ever-changing world of the finite with the magnificent real world of the Infinite.

Your Reason for Being on Earth

Your reason for being in earth's schoolroom is first and foremost that you develop by your free-will consent the masterful qualities that are a part of the character and being of God. When God created you in his image and likeness, he endowed you with his eternal flame. This flame was and is the very essence of himself, and because he gave it to you it is also the essence of yourself. Now pause and meditate on this truth.

Consider that when God gave you the gift of his flame, he gave you the gift of himself. He anchored that very flame, that divine spark, in your heart. And there he keeps his vigil with you from your first breath to your last. Accept this truth as a spiritually scientific fact and dwell forevermore in his eternal flame and in his Divine Self.

The Great Spirit is all-goodness and all-intelligence. As a spirit-spark of the Great Spirit, you were created to internalize his all-goodness and his all-intelligence.

Mirror the Character of Your Divine Self

But lifetime after lifetime, many of you have severely limited the expression of your innate God-goodness and your innate God-intelligence. You have set up self-limiting karmic patterns. You have planted a hedge around your backyard, and there you sit hedging life's options but never exercising any of them. You have sometimes even responded negatively to life's opportunities carved out specifically for you by your spiritual mentors.

Thus, your Divine Self has restrained your use of his power. And he will continue to restrain your use of his power until such time as you elect by your free will to develop your character in the similitude of his character.

Day by day, as you assemble the building blocks of his character and make them your own, you will know an inner strength coupled with a fierce determination to do the will of your Divine Self. Then you yourself will restrain your uses of God's power. And by and by, you will prove not only to yourself but to your Divine Self that you can hold the reins of self-discipline in the uses of power under the most trying and provocative circumstances. Then you will lawfully receive God's power, as well as his empowerment of your spirit.

Moreover, when you accomplish your soul's mirroring of the character of your Divine Self, you will become a transparency for his eternal virtues and moral values. God's thoughts will become your thoughts, God's words will become your words and God's deeds will become your deeds.

When your thoughts, words and deeds become wholly the reflection of your Divine Self, you will be found worthy of exercising divine power even in spiritual dimensions of your being. Then we, your mentors, will signal you that you have passed a major hurdle on the path of your soul's initiations.

Remember the Patterns of Perfection

There is no competition in God. He delights in the diversity of his creation, for he conceived of the patterns in the heavens and the patterns in the earth after the nature of his own being. Patterns and patterning establish the foundations of worlds within and worlds without.

The creation was patterned by God in the beginning of this cosmic cycle. And in the ending he will roll up the scrolls of his patternings and cast them into the sacred fire, only to repeat the process in the next cosmic cycle and the next.

Whether or not we attain to a state of permanence in God in this cosmic cycle (as in heaven, so on earth) has to do with the patterns we ourselves overlay on our four lower bodies—in our very souls, minds, bodies and especially in our desires. Some patterns will be of the heavenly, but most will be of the earth, earthy. For centuries have faded into the mists of aeons and we scarcely remember the patterns of perfection upon which we once built our lives and civilizations.

And so, here below, prior to our soul's reunion with God, we are the self-made prisoners of our own karmic patterns. For the most part, our souls, sullied by these patterns, mirror neither the original pristine patterns of Eden nor the heavenly patterns that gave birth to that paradise. Yet, it is all-important to remember that our souls and our four lower bodies must merge with those patterns if we are to enter the realms of eternal life, nevermore to depart from the patterns of our original birthright in God.

God Desires Your Happiness

The LORD God does not desire to perpetuate the judgment he pronounced upon Adam and Eve and other twin flames who were students in the ancient mystery school called Eden. It is man himself who has perpetuated the judgment through self-punishment and his belief in the lie of eternal damnation that has been foisted upon him by the fallen angels.

Jesus Christ referred to these reprobate angels as wolves in sheep's clothing. So they were and so they are. And to this day they continue to spread abroad their philosophy of hellfire and damnation.

God does not desire to prolong man's unhappiness. Nor would he see him flagellate himself for sins he has long forgiven and forgotten. Nor would he extend man's state of imperfection indefinitely. When man himself shares God's desires, he will no longer see himself as unhappy, sinful or imperfect.

But until man does share God's desires for him, the Divine Self has established his guardianship over him, putting in place necessary safeguards and restraints, including setting the clamp on his mortality at three-score and ten. This limitation of the average life span was set to prevent the perpetuation of undesirable traits of mortal thought and feeling.

You are responsible for bringing your own abundant life into manifestation. Once you have developed your attunement with the mind of Christ, this process will take place as naturally as a flower unfolds her petals. For the Christ acts as a mediator between your soul and your Divine Self and imputes to you that understanding of righteousness which translates as your right use of the Law under the Father's will.

Pride Prevents Spiritual Progress

The dark ones have employed many weapons to keep the children of the Light from discovering the Real Self. The most darkening of all such weapons is the screen of egoistic, self-centeredness including that altogether human quality of pride, which so readily saturates individual self-awareness. Beloved ones, pride is so subtle that people often mistake it for spiritual zeal.

The Great Doer is the Eternal One, who would fully employ humanity—heart, head and hand—but never without individual consent. His intent is to turn over to the soul the full employment of her God-given talents just as soon as she has demonstrated her self-worth and her capacity to receive them.

The soul's correct use of her God-given talents, multiplied by her diligence in their application, is always carried out under the direction of the genius that God has implanted in her consciousness. Each soul has access to this "genius pool," but she must activate it by walking in the footsteps of her spiritual mentors. And herein lies the key to her self-transcendence.

If the soul would embrace the Infinite One through the chain of the spiritual hierarchy of this planet, she must subordinate herself to the ascended masters who will lead her on an ascending staircase to the source of being. Only by so doing shall she be vested with the mysteries of God and his spiritual genius.

This genius is not to be compared to the genius of the human mind. Nay, the genius of which we speak takes the soul in a giant leap from the finite mind to the infinite mind of God. The soul has access to that higher mind only when she has surrendered the finite mind to the Eternal One so that he may do with it what he will.

With all of their hearts, men should guard their consciousness against the Luciferian attitude of human pride. With few exceptions, the people evolving upon this planet have lurking within their consciousness the quality of pride which shows its face when individuals allow themselves to become piqued over little things.

The spiritually progressive person who is willing to engage in a bit of introspection should note when he becomes annoyed or angry with others over trifles or unimportant matters that ought not to make any difference. These are indications of personal pride. One should learn balance and reasonability, giving to others the same grace that one expects to receive.

Self-Control of the Emotions

Through inward delight in the law of God,[1] man can reach the point where he is able to withstand the onslaughts of excess emotionalism and hold himself in the balance of the universal light, even when his sensitive nature causes him to feel the pain of anger or regret concerning the conduct of another. Self-control of the emotions and the feeling world is one of the keys to self-mastery which some of our disciples find difficult to employ.

Because the individual identifies with his consciousness, he is sensitive to circumstances which invade his consciousness and which he may interpret as an affront to his own life. By identifying with all life right while he maintains an awareness of his personal function and a sense of his personal mission, he can easily understand why individuals may act or react as they do.

This understanding will spread the oil of tranquillity on the troubled waters of human affairs. Above all, the self should remain poised yet not aloof or without compassion for the problems of others.

The Brotherhood advocates training in sensitivity

to Christ, but we would point out that psychic sensitizing and improper physical contact with others (which comes under the heading of "sensitivity training") is a dangerous procedure which can very easily bring about the demise of needed individuality.

The Dignity of True Self-Realization

Men need to preserve the individual self while they attain spiritual identification with the Real Self. Expanding that sense of identification, one can include as a part of his own self-awareness the God Presence in all life. And he need not explore the human psyche or physique in order to achieve this awareness.

Effective God-control over the creation must be maintained in the universe so that God can produce the reality of his kingdom everywhere. Where the Spirit is not present, where the Spirit is denied, where the Spirit is quenched,[2] there is no fount of reality that brings the buoyancy of interspiritual and interpersonal realizations to the consciousness.

The little bursts of joy that flood the soul as it comes in contact with those who are spiritually of like mind is a certain indication of the presence of the Holy Spirit. Those who engage in so-called mental karate, those who seek to control or to hypnotize others, often do not realize that they are functioning outside of the eternal

Father's intent. Each son or daughter of God, in the dignity of true self-realization, must hold a sense of his or her own individual mission and expand outward in consciousness through the heavenly Presence to understand the life plan of others.

In one sense, all life is one. And this is the highest sense. But in the lower senses there are many snares and tangles to be avoided. Through discretion, Christ-discrimination and holy prayer, men retain their divine dignity, which does not preclude the possibility of the effervescing of the self in humor and perpetual joyousness. Such dignity is never overcome by person, place, condition or thing.

Become the Fullness of All That Is Real

Health, faith and determination are all adjuncts to the expansion of the real in man. You must come each day to a greater understanding of yourself in order to be able to rightly represent the purposes of life. You are love and you love love. You are wisdom and you love wisdom. You are power and you love power.

But you know that all is fulfilled in the perfect triangle of balanced attitude. This is the attitude that seeks the commonweal and understands the dangers of mental manipulation. Through human cleverness and wit, the kingdom of God has suffered violence,[3] the world order has been tampered with and the forces of the media have been used for purposes of negative control.

The key to the redemption of the social system lies in the victory of divine law in the being of individual man. What the individual man becomes, the collective world is.

Wholeheartedly enter into the kingdom of God and his righteousness.[4] And participate in those spiritual exercises that strip you of the false and clothe you with the real. You and your world, then, can and must become the fullness of all that God intended from the beginning.

O wisdom's star, continue to shine!

Graciously, I AM

Lanto

6

Energy Levels and the Potential of the Self

If you want to awaken all of humanity,
then awaken all of yourself.

LAO TZU

In order to create a crystal-clear picture of the self, we shall discuss the self in terms of energy levels. The parable of the talents reveals that individuals vary according to the gifts given to them. As Jesus Christ said:

The kingdom of heaven is as a man travelling into a far country, who called his own servants and delivered unto them his goods.

And unto one he gave five talents, to another two and to another one; to every man according to his several ability; and straightway took his journey.

Then he that had received the five talents went and traded with the same and made them other five talents.

And likewise he that had received two, he also gained other two.

But he that had received one went and digged in the earth and hid his lord's money.

After a long time the lord of those servants cometh and reckoneth with them.

And so he that had received five talents came and brought other five talents, saying, "Lord, thou deliveredst unto me five talents. Behold, I have gained beside them five talents more."

His lord said unto him, "Well done, thou good and faithful servant. Thou hast been faithful over a few things; I will make thee ruler over many things. Enter thou into the joy of thy lord."

He also that had received two talents came and said, "Lord, thou deliveredst unto me two talents. Behold, I have gained two other talents beside them."

His lord said unto him, "Well done, good and faithful servant. Thou hast been faithful over a few things; I will make thee ruler over many things. Enter thou into the joy of thy lord."

Then he which had received the one talent came and said, "Lord, I knew thee that thou art an hard man, reaping where thou hast not sown and gathering where thou hast not strawed:

"And I was afraid and went and hid thy talent in the earth. Lo, there thou hast that is thine."

His lord answered and said unto him, "Thou wicked and slothful servant, thou knewest that I reap where I sowed not and gather where I have not strawed:

"Thou oughtest therefore to have put my money to the exchangers, and then at my coming I should have received mine own with usury.

"Take therefore the talent from him and give it unto him which hath ten talents.

"For unto every one that hath shall be given, and he shall have abundance: but from him that hath not shall be taken away even that which he hath.

"And cast ye the unprofitable servant into outer darkness: there shall be weeping and gnashing of teeth."[1]

This is also true of energy levels. Health, karma and aspiration are among the many factors that govern the abundance of energy one has at his disposal. Energy levels also vary within the framework of a norm—a high and a low.

Karma Governs Soul Energy

Most people don't realize that the potential of the self is related to the quantity and quality of the energy which they use. If you will think of the nature of the soul as the nature of God and consider that (1) God is boundless energy, (2) man has been given a limited quantity of God's energy and (3) the energy which man has been given comprises the content of the soul, you will be on the right track in your investigations of the self.

Jesus warned that men could lose their souls. He said: "And fear not them which kill the body but are not able to kill the soul. But rather fear him which is able to destroy both soul and body in hell."[2] For what is a man advantaged if he gain the whole world and lose himself or become a castaway?

Many trials and taxing situations may deplete the amount of energy available to a given individual. I do not say that all energy used by man comes from the soul, for as you know man's supply comes from the Holy Spirit. As the apostle James wrote, "Every good gift and every perfect gift is from above and cometh down from the Father of lights, with whom is no variableness, neither shadow of turning."[3]

But I do relate soul energy to the temporal manifestation of identity. This soul energy, or solar energy, is limited in quantity—some having a great deal more of it than others. As a man soweth, so shall he also reap.[4] Therefore, karma acts as the governor, in part, of the flow of man's energy from his God Presence, just as it regulates the amount of soul energy given to the lifestream at the beginning of each embodiment.

Health is related to karma, and both are cumulative. Health is the result of man's past and present uses of energy. Good health encourages the steadfast flow of energy through the four lower bodies. The reverse is also true.

The Right Use of Energy Increases It

We cannot deny that there are good and bad energies. But let us remember that energy itself is really neither good nor bad; it is the qualification that determines its inherent manifestation.

Therefore, in our study we must remember to relate energy and its qualification to the self. An initial impetus or quantity of energy is bestowed upon the individual as his divine portion. This is brought out in the parable of the prodigal son.[5]

The statement "To him that hath shall be given, and he shall have abundance: but from him that hath not shall be taken away even that which he hath"[6] also gives a clue to the maintenance of the energy potential necessary to the self—what we might call the "critical mass."

The more energy a person has, the more energy he is apt to attract; the less he has, the less he is apt to attract. The need to purify one's energies becomes more and more apparent as the individual sees that his life potential is dependent upon the quality of his energy.

Actually, a great deal of energy which was once his to use is now imprisoned in the imperfect patterns of his own human miscreations. Like money in the bank which has been pledged as collateral, this energy cannot be withdrawn until one's spiritual obligations have been met.

Release Yourself from Tensions

Those who serve mankind in the field of medicine understand that when tension builds up in the muscle groups of the body, a great amount of energy is held there and this affects the entire body. They know that the release of tension in the muscles provides more energy for both mind and body.

Likewise, those who understand the human mind know that emotionally tying up the psyche with diverse problems can cause a split personality. Increased mental and emotional tensions create a buildup of attracting and repelling forces that divide the self. Continual fatigue can also lead to a much greater tendency toward mental disorders.

What man must do, then, is to learn how to release himself from tensions—physically, mentally and emotionally. He must learn to use all of the energy which God has given him, some of which is in a state of rest and some of which is in motion.

He must learn to undo the misqualifications of energy for which he bears responsibility. He must learn to requalify the energy that has been misqualified. This will give him a greater quotient of energy that can be used in the development of true soul consciousness, for the purposes of life involve man mastering the universe by first mastering himself.

Draw upon the Energy of Your Higher Nature

In a very real sense, the spiritual energies of the divine image are reflected in the mirror of mortal consciousness. These energies bring about the advent of soul force within the lifestream, but they must be continuously augmented so that the expanding soul may attract a greater portion of divinity to the life of the individual.

All undesirable karmic manifestations return to

their point of origin—which is the individual being of man—when the attractive force within him, whether qualified with good or ill, has reached a certain intensity. Therefore, it is well that individuals recognize that when they draw to themselves the higher nature of being, they are also drawing a definitive quantity as well as a definitive quality of energy. That energy will fortify the being of man against the day of karmic reckoning when all negatives and positives must be adjusted, and he must rise or fall before his Creator.

In our considerations of man's energy potential we are concerned with both quality and quantity. The Absolute is all and therefore possesses all (and in a sense is possessed by all). Thus, all energy ever entrusted to your soul must eventually return to its source.

The universal desire for purity in the self—whether it is the desire of the macrocosmic Lord of the universe or the desire of the individual monad—spurs a progressive outreach for more and more of the reality of right qualification. As you think of the soul as the repository of the energies of the fiery world,[7] you will feel a greater sense of responsibility to maintain the soul and its contents upon the altar of purity.

And perhaps you will consider more often how vastly beneficial it will be—not only to you as an individual but also to the universe as a whole—if you will learn how to summon the will to requalify negative thoughts, feelings and creations with the pristine beauty of the first creation of God. Think of the worlds of misqualified substance that are waiting to be conquered when you practice the supreme art of transmutation as taught by Saint Germain.[8]

Following the ascended master Jesus Christ in the regeneration, cradling the infant Messiah in the crèche of the heart, men will begin the process of expanding their understanding of self through becoming all that is real and discarding, through requalification, all that is unreal.

Become as a Little Child

This task may seem interminable and the process involved, but it is not. Except ye become as a little child, ye cannot enter in.

> And they brought young children to him, that he should touch them: and his disciples rebuked those that brought them.
>
> But when Jesus saw it, he was much displeased and said unto them, "Suffer the little children to come unto me and forbid them not, for of such is the kingdom of God.
>
> "Verily I say unto you, Whosoever shall not

receive the kingdom of God as a little child, he shall not enter therein."

And he took them up in his arms, put his hands upon them and blessed them.[9]

To manifest the little-child consciousness is to develop the masterful Christ consciousness that through the Holy Spirit will ultimately take dominion over the earth.[10]

Wait, watch and work. For the Father works with you and within you.

Faithfully, I AM your brother,

Kuthumi

7

The Ego

"How are you?"
"Perfect, thank you. I'm traveling incognito."
"Oh? As what are you disguised?"
"I am disguised as myself."
"Don't be silly. That's no disguise. That's what you are."
"On the contrary, it must be a very good disguise,
for I see it has fooled you completely."

NASRUDIN

When functioning properly, consciousness is a glowing orb of reality, joy and full illumination. The individual who reaches out from the seemingly separated center of being can, if he will, contact the cosmic center of life. From there he may reach out to the periphery of all reality as easily as the miracle of the radiant, expanding mind of God penetrates the universe with light.

Inherent within man is the power to expand

consciousness beyond the sphere of the personal self into the domain of universal reality shared by the myriad manifestations that inhabit cosmos. The marvelous quality of "locked-in individuality" never oppresses the permanent nature of man. Consciousness unfolds and the gentle molding factors of the hand of universal intelligence, power and love tutor the evolving soul personality.

Soul Renewal

As beloved Kuthumi has said, individuals may easily misqualify energy. On the other hand, they may just as easily begin to requalify energy. Thus, people of any age can look forward to experiencing newness of life and a sense of fulfillment not known before. Soon they will bypass the structures that they have created and that have been created for them by the dark overlords and their dark stars of compounded misqualification.

Souls will realize, with the joy of a newborn babe, that the universe is a home of light and hope. It is a place where the temporal manifestations of intelligence can be welded to the Eternal, even as the Eternal permeates the substance of mortality with its essential reality. Mankind, then, can come to know the permanent gift of bliss which the Father-Mother God joyously conveyed to their offspring at the birth of their identity.

The ocean could have chosen to remain the ocean, but by separating the tiny luminous drop from the whole and holding it up to the glorious rays of the sun of illumination, a new ocean was begun. And so the individual consciousness was given dominion over his own world. Man, made in the image of his Creator,[1] became a creator in his own right.

Egoistic Expression Creates a Sense of Struggle

The first stirrings of reality outside of the lost Edenic state moved in the darkness, in the void of unknowing. These stirrings of purpose were soon translated into outer action, but the fabrications of social contact unfortunately dedicated themselves to egoistic expression and a sense of struggle.

Man's rise seemed to be proportionate to his dominion, not over self but over others and over his environment. The overcoming of environment was valid. The wreaking of destruction upon others was not. Therefore, the divine tribunal of justice known as the Karmic Board came into being in order to record and govern the interaction of man's humanity or inhumanity to man.

The sense of struggle mounted. Involvement in the ego became a snarl of inverted spirals, structuring within the consciousness of mankind a kaleidoscopic reverie so complex as to make the consciousness recoil.

The simple forms of grace were forgotten in the astral melodrama. Man seemed to live without, but actually he lived within the snares of his own creation. Now he was infecting others with his own dilemma, and the power of contagion banished him from the heavenly state.

How to Escape the Illusory Self

The ego is the seat of all man's problems. What are known as inferiority or superiority complexes revolve entirely around the pride and frustration of the ego. But although people know these things, they continue to allow themselves to be victimized by the internal obstructions which they have created.

The only way out is through the door of reality. This is the escape hatch which has been provided to mankind so that the body of destructivity created by man's own negativity can be transmuted and overcome. As long as men remain involved in the ego—no matter what religious study they undertake, no matter what devotion they temporarily manifest, no matter how many good works they do, no matter what level of striving they attain to—they will never be free from the illusion of the self that pursues them as a wanton ghost of struggling identity.

They will begin to know the freedom of the self to

achieve without limit only when they escape through the door ("I AM the door"[2]) into the understanding that the eternal being of God is the "doer." Then they will realize that God can act in them to remove hampering influences, to transmute their darkness and to translate their consciousness from darkness into light.

Gaze Honestly into the Mirror of Self

We could set up guidelines which would help you to recognize when the ego is in command, but I think that a little honest gazing into the mirror of self and a study of the reactions of the self to the doings of others will quickly show, if one's appraisal be honest, whether or not the ego is acting.

Let all see and know for all eternity that the not-self, the shadowed-self, the named-self, the personality-self, is and always has been the snare of the ego and that the man or woman who lives in that consciousness must die in it. There is no possibility for flesh and blood to inherit eternal life.[3]

Men seek eternal life because it is their true nature, the nature of God and of the divine image. Eternal life is formed independently of the vehicle of self through the process of translation, that man should no longer see death but be translated into that life which is the divine nature.

The saying that man should die daily[4] to the finite, egoistic self must be followed by another statement— that he should live daily to the progressive glory of his eternal God Self and the apprehending of all the reality which that Self can and does bring. This is the sun we face that casts no shadow.

Oh, we can and we will bring forth such an abundant wealth of spiritual information regarding the true nature of man as to almost consume man's present consciousness. Yet we must delay until man has had ample opportunity to understand that he must shed the ego.

This concept is far more than a stream of words. It is a flow of the vital seed-idea into the consciousness of man whereby consciousness itself is transformed into its natural glowing Presence. This is the Presence of God, which identifies the individual through his sense of expanding reality with the universal consciousness of God. Yet it never takes from him one erg of his energy or of his true selfhood.

Replace the Vain Intellect with the Mind of God

The Father created the Son to be the beloved inheritor of all things that were made. And in reality the Son of God, who is the light of God that never fails, was the means by which the Eternal Progenitor performed the creative act. "Thou art my beloved Son, in whom I am well pleased."[5]

The ego that is always being hurt, that is over-sensitive, full of self-pity and the sense of struggle, the ego that seeks in poring over the rubble of past lives to find some element of worth should understand that man's worth is in the light of the Eternal Now. He should appreciate that the Eternal Now is in the Eternal and that the grace that man must have that is sufficient for every day was implanted within the soul with the inpouring breath of divine energy that first gave him consciousness.

In the name of holy wisdom I, Meru, urge upon everyone the willful relinquishing of the snakeskin of identity that has crawled upon its belly while pursuing the vanities of the intellect. Replace this by the dominant sunburst of the living, vital mind of God and that reality which God is and which you are because he *is*.

I AM his servant and your elder brother,

Meru

8

Spreading the Network of Joy

> When people see the habitual
> happiness in your eyes, it will make them
> realize they are the loved children of God....
> Joy is very infectious; therefore,
> be always full of joy.
>
> MOTHER TERESA

Our subject is the spreading of the network of joy, the antithesis of sorrow, in the domain of consciousness and communicating it into the world of form. When the individual monad can willingly give up the personal self in a genuine act of surrender, he is soon magnetized to the God-ideal of spreading into the world the marvelous activity of vibrant joy—joy in self, in nature, in opportunity, in service, in music and art, and even joy in the process of purifying the self.

Every facet of life is a challenge to those who daily

strive to be more like God. This is not a challenge of discomfort but of hope. The fact that the individual can
improve regardless of his station, that he can change his
vibration and the contents of his mind as he would his
garments is a sign of hope and a portent of delight.

Energy fields can be magnificent when they are
properly qualified. For not only can they surround their
creator with his own vibration of bliss but, according to
the law of attraction, they can also magnetize the vibrations of joy and happiness from many parts of the world.

Be Aware of What You Attract to Your World

We acknowledge that the reverse is also true. Seldom
do people realize that from time to time they are surrounded with discarnate entities—entities of fear, of doubt
and of grief. Individuals create the climate that attracts
these outsiders into their aura by their own attitudes.

A discarnate entity is a disembodied spirit who has
not ascended to God; hence he is not karma-free nor is
he free from the wheel of rebirth. Since such a soul has
not passed through the ritual of the ascension and
become fully God-identified, he is as subject to error as
anyone in embodiment. Still possessed of elements of a
human ego as well as momentums of negativity, he may
transmit these intentionally or unintentionally.

Discarnate entities may be benign, but they are not

omniscient. They may impart truth, but they can be opinionated, proud and self-seeking. They are known to use people to achieve their own ends even as they steal people's light.

Discarnate entities consume vital soul energies, draining the channeler as well as those present of the spiritual essence necessary to true progress on the Path. Some well-known channelers say they are exhausted after their channeling sessions, and many people report feeling depleted after attending a séance.

By contrast, the energy released by the God-free ascended beings who speak from the highest octaves of light, one with the universal mind, is stupendous. It is exhilarating. It charges and recharges the body, mind and spirit of each person in the congregation. It clears the chakras and draws the soul nigh to her own inner God-reality.

Discover the Cause of Your Moods

In the matter of moods, we would suggest to every student that whenever he is invaded by feelings that are less than God-happiness—feelings of discomfort or disquietude—that he look for the cause of those feelings in his own subconscious mind. This may include his entertaining negative ideas which may have entered his world.

Second, he should consider the influence of masquerading or malevolent entities. When an individual seeks to improve himself by engaging in religious worship, by attending a constructive lecture or concert, or by reading religious literature, the vibratory action of the higher pursuit makes any invading entities he may be harboring extremely uncomfortable.

Thus the entities, unwilling to relinquish their hold on the lifestream, will project to his consciousness a feeling of discomfort or unhappiness. The entities will assure the individual that this is directly attributable to the activity in which he is involved.

In this manner, many sincere souls are either stopped on the Path or they are prevented from obtaining the benefits of higher meditation. Thus, through their susceptibility to invading entities, they are deprived of the opportunity to receive transcendent blessings.

The Need for Protection on the Spiritual Path

This is why spiritual protection is necessary for those who would continue to progress on the upward way. And I speak of protection not only through the knowledge I am conveying but also through decrees, through prayer and through the determination to do the will of God no matter what.

Thus, you will find yourself making rapid spiritual progress when you determine to cast out discarnate entities from your world. These include departed spirits of relatives, friends or enemies. And they may be positively or negatively magnetized to your person.

Indeed, invoking God's protection will insulate you from the malice of those whom you may not even know are your enemies. This malice often comes through practitioners of black magic, witchcraft and Satanism who use their powers to attack those who would escape their influence. These practices can be subtly alluring to those not grounded in spiritual knowledge and who do not understand the karmic penalties that accrue from such dangerous activities.

Because of the increasing threat of witchcraft, black magic and Satanism in the United States and throughout the world, spiritual aspirants must exercise caution and discern when negative influences are acting in their worlds. They should always weigh the evidence before they credit their failures or seeming failures to themselves.[1]

Self-Defeating Activities

When spiritual aspirants become aware of their progress on the Path, they may find that they must also grapple with an inflated ego. On the other hand, they may find themselves envying the supposed progress of others. Jesus described this human propensity in his statement "Woe unto you, lawyers! For ye have taken away the key of knowledge: ye entered not in yourselves, and them that were entering in ye hindered."[2]

Many in the orthodox churches are naive to these influences. They are entirely too standpat in matters of the self. Quite frankly, as you have been told in this series, the self is little understood.

This is why people often work against their own best interests and against the best interests of humanity. It is why they are so easily captivated by the idea of massive social gain and why the dark forces are able to create so much unrest in the world.

Many do not understand that God-power and God-control come only from a higher power. They think that they can gain spiritually as well as materially through coercion and government control.

On the contrary, the ideal society evolves out of higher consciousness when the individual opens the door of his being to God without reserve. In moments of personal contact with God, the entire being of man becomes as a mouth pressing itself against the Infinite in order to receive the subtle nourishment that floods into the hungry soul.

Let Your Higher Self Guide You

Because the grace that comes from on high is so creative, so inspirational, so expansive, it literally overwhelms the being of man. Spilling over the lip of life's chalice, it floods forth as the impulse to benefit the race. Such impulses must be channeled constructively to protect oneself and help others realize their highest nature.

Each one must realize that the higher intelligence within himself is capable of making accurate decisions as to when he should speak and when he should be silent, when he should offer a helping hand and when he should withhold it. There are times when nothing is as important as a gesture of assistance to another. But at other times, such a gesture may be dangerous. Some of the best gifts that can be given are inner gifts such as the communication of comfort, hope and joy.

Consciousness should be as a grail, for the knowledge that flows into that grail draws more and more of the regenerative Christ into the domain of the self. Certainly it is true that if a man ask of God bread, he will not give him a stone.[3]

Therefore, consider that constructive endeavor always receives the necessary support spiritually, morally and materially. And the more man spiritually accepts the highest sense of his mission, the greater that support will be.

The Soul's Need for Grace

"It is more blessed to give than to receive."[4] Yet unless men receive, they cannot give. Therefore, the soul's allotted portion must be understood as the grace of God on deposit in the great Causal Body of each individual.

As man is able to receive the judgments of God, he can grow in grace and in the knowledge of truth. And tomorrow he can become a greater servant than he is today by multiplying what he has received. This continual flow of God's grace through his being is all-important. For if man becomes an inlet with no outlet, he will eventually become a parasite on the world body.

The foundation stones of the temple must be laid while consciousness is held in readiness. This is accomplished when the seeker of God's will does whatever is necessary to further the kingdom of God both within and without.

Man must qualify his energy with divine love just as the pulsing joy of God vivaciously entices all of Mother Nature to perform her wondrous feats. Her miracles of temporal reality are immortalized even as they are recycled.

The Spiritual Interchange Between God and Man

In like manner, the individual shall one day realize the true meaning of his life in the spiritual interchange between the microcosm and the macrocosm. Through this process the allness of man flows into the allness of God, and the allness of God flows into the allness of man. This brings about an exchange of the pulsations of identity which transform the soul as she bows in joyous humility before the living God.

Truly "he hath put down the mighty from their seats and exalted them of low degree."[5] Truly the living God is crowned in every atom. Truly each man is the son of the Eternal One. Move on, then, to understand that which you can be. For out of the expectancy of hope is born the faith that establishes the borders of self where charity dwells.

When the meaning of true love is known, it is found to re-create that supreme moment when the innocent soul cried out with divine wonder, "Because thou art, O God, I AM!" Thus we see the links of identity, intelligence, power and love uniting all to the oneness that is God.

Victoriously, I remain

Lanto

9

"It Does Not Matter!"

As a drop of water
does not stick to a lotus leaf or as
a lotus flower is untainted by the water,
so the sage does not cling to anything—
seen, heard or thought.

GAUTAMA BUDDHA

"It does not matter!" When you can say that to the unavoidable circumstance and commit the keeping of yourself unto God without reserve, you are truly beginning to come out of the bondage of Egypt. (For Egypt symbolizes the material creation—the pyramid of matter standing by the ever-flowing Nile of time, winding through the sand of space.) You feel no qualms of anguish because, to the best of your ability, you have sought and held to your Higher Self even while understanding the need to surrender the sense of self-righteousness.

When the fiery world of the Holy Spirit is revealed more fully to embodied men and women, they are able to grasp the real meaning of life. This glorious realm possesses consciousness even as it produces material form, primal substance and secondary creation.

Those who perceive the fiery world see the schoolrooms of earth, the geometric corners of creation, the endless circles of repetitious activities and the noble aspirations of triadic manifestation. And they recognize their inner need to obtain congruency with reality. But when they understand that the tensions of spiritual determination are necessary reinforcements in the battle of overcoming the transitory, they are on the road to victory. Yet we must map out the campaign long before we are able to execute it.

Freedom from Self-Imposed Bondage

One of the saddest facts of human existence is that some people, by reason of their own self-importance and materialistic insensibilities, reject the necessary instructions that would have given them their freedom not only in some ultimate time but also in the here and now. Instead they allow themselves to remain tethered to the bondage that has continuously caused their joys to be spilled from the cup of life.

But heaven is both subjective and objective. Therefore, the cry has gone forth that many who are first shall be last and that the last shall be first.[1]

Let men see to it that they lose not the crown of their rejoicing.[2] Temporal life is without bond or guarantee and can be terminated at any time. The business of acquiring spiritual fortitude and spiritual reality is the only business in which the soul ought to be engaged.

Without realizing what they are doing, countless individuals spurn genuine activities of the Holy Spirit that would enable their souls to grow fat. Instead they have chosen to revel in the entertainment marts of the world or in psychic phenomena.

There are enough rewards in true spirituality to warrant men placing their attention upon the higher teachings. Like the proverbial pot of gold at the end of the rainbow, these teachings have consistently drawn men to the gold of their Higher Self. And I am certain you know that all is not gold that glitters in the field of so-called esoteric studies. But pray you must if you would be free from self-imposed bondage. And in so doing, recognize the potential you have to endow the nations with immortal freedom.

The World Hungers for Personal and Spiritual Freedom

The way of the Christ is the way of life, truth and love. It is the way of faith, hope and charity. The ascended masters are not dead. God is not dead. Hope is not dead. And even in man's darkest hour, freedom itself is not dead so long as the freedom to produce the vibration of virtue and valor and aspiration lives perpetually within the soul.

The freedoms of speech, religion, the press and the right to assemble are necessary so that God and man might have the opportunity to communicate the living Christ to the world. Moreover, in order to break the bread of the knowledge of one's True Self to humanity, man must be able to disseminate that bread of knowledge.

Where these freedoms are forbidden by law or men are harassed by those who think they do God's service when they interfere with the flow of the highest truth, millions are deprived of their rightful inheritance. For this reason, the ascended masters have sought to incorporate into the American dream a dream of freedom that can and should be patterned by all nations. For the people of the world hunger for personal freedom as well as for spiritual freedom.

Men have no more loyal or devoted friends anywhere than among the ascended masters. Yet we also acknowledge our friendship with a host of patriots who live yet in the veil of flesh as servants of God and friends of all mankind. These will not permit themselves to be blown by the wind as chaff.[3]

These patriots insist on the dignity of their worth, of their service, of their lives and of the pursuits which God has made for all to enjoy. They see the vehicle of the little self as expendable, even as they know that their greatest strength emanates from their dedication to spiritual goals.

Choose Liberating Friendships

Matter and substance change. The individual's consciousness is altered by planetary circumstance, by education, by interactions within the family, by economic levels, by his intelligence quotient and through associations with others. Consider, then, the meaning of choosing one's friends carefully.

If some of your friends are turning you against God, if their thoughts are destroying your peace of mind, if their activities are a constant war against your spirit, regardless of how close they may be to you, you might ask yourself this question: In the name of Almighty God, should these friends remain a permanent part of my life or should I make room for more liberating friendships?

Only you can determine what course to take. But it would be well to remember what Jesus said long ago, "He that loveth father or mother more than me is not worthy of me, and he that loveth son or daughter more than me is not worthy of me."[4]

If the Christ sought to save men's lives, why would he ask them to deny their lives or those of their families before him? The question simply becomes, What is real and what is unreal?

Surrender to God Is Life, Not Death

The Christ image of every man which was bestowed upon him by God is real. The self that must be denied is unreal. The unreal self seeks to cramp the style of the real, to hold it in bondage. And so Ishmael, the son of Hagar, the bondwoman, is not to be compared with the Son of promise.[5]

The altar of being in the world of form is the threshing floor of the Most High. The flailing of the grain is the chastening of God that refines the pure gold of the soul and brings it to the surface where it can be gathered into the treasure-house of reality. Many who read about reality fail to realize their responsibility to make the best use of the opportunities which life extends to them while they are in embodiment.

Surrender to God is life, not death. It is the beatification of the soul. It is hope. It is the wings of the mind borne upward into the lightness of celestial realities. No empty void is there. The natives of cosmos in all of their blazing reality—ministering spirits, angels, cosmic beings, cosmic masters, one and all—as the higher kin of every man, hold their offerings of eternal sweetness for the purification and release of the souls of men from bondage.

What a wonderful schoolhouse the planet earth is! How joyously people can chuckle in the midst of their misfortunes even when long shadows cross their paths.

Men must learn to shatter their human bondage and to regard it as an enemy. They must see the clutching of the little self as a frightening thing, for in one moment it could cause them to drown in a sea of troubles. On the other hand, the lifeline to the Higher Self is already flung out. And the eternal Presence waits as the Father draws the prodigal son of the little self into the mooring of his eternal greatness.

Spiritual Rebirth

Whether one has attained his victory yesterday or today or whether one will do so in the near future, when it comes it is the long-awaited product of the soul's eternal evolution. And in a very real sense, it is a spiritual rebirth.

There was a man of the Pharisees named Nicodemus, a ruler of the Jews:

The same came to Jesus by night and said unto him, "Rabbi, we know that thou art a teacher come from God, for no man can do these miracles that thou doest except God be with him."

Jesus answered and said unto him, "Verily, verily, I say unto thee, Except a man be born again, he cannot see the kingdom of God."

Nicodemus saith unto him, "How can a man be born when he is old? Can he enter the second time into his mother's womb and be born?"

Jesus answered, "Verily, verily, I say unto thee, Except a man be born of water and of the [Holy] Spirit, he cannot enter into the kingdom of God.

"That which is born of the flesh is flesh, and that which is born of the [Holy] Spirit is spirit.

"Marvel not that I said unto thee, Ye must be born again.

"The wind bloweth where it listeth, and thou hearest the sound thereof but canst not tell whence it cometh and whither it goeth: so is every one that is born of the [Holy] Spirit."

Nicodemus answered and said unto him, "How can these things be?"

Jesus answered and said unto him, "Art thou a master of Israel and knowest not these things?

"Verily, verily, I say unto thee, We speak that we do know and testify that we have seen, and ye receive not our witness.

"If I have told you earthly things and ye believe not, how shall ye believe if I tell you of heavenly things?

"And no man hath ascended up to heaven but he that came down from heaven, even the Son of man which is in heaven.

"And as Moses lifted up the serpent in the wilderness, even so must the Son of man be lifted up:

"That whosoever believeth in him should not perish, but have eternal life.

"For God so loved the world, that he gave his only begotten Son, that whosoever believeth in him should not perish but have everlasting life.

"For God sent not his Son into the world to condemn the world but that the world through him might be saved.

"He that believeth on him is not condemned: but he that believeth not is condemned already, because he hath not believed in the name of the only begotten Son of God.

"And this is the condemnation, that light is come into the world, and men loved darkness rather than light because their deeds were evil.

"For every one that doeth evil hateth the light, neither cometh to the light lest his deeds should be reproved.

"But he that doeth truth cometh to the light, that his deeds may be made manifest that they are wrought in God."[6]

These words signify that man is not only of the earth, earthy but that he is also a product of his heavenly aspirations.[7]

Identify with the Hopes of God

God hopes for the soul. Man must identify with the hopes of God. And then as the tolling of a great bell, the death knell of the finite self will make no mournful sound, but it will sing to the soul in cadences of immortality.

Through these cadences, man shall come to understand the golden meaning of reality, and the revelation of worlds unknown shall also be his own. Stretching as an endless column of beautiful trees, the landmarks of the real point the way from present circumstances to the very footstool of reality, the rainbow of ascendancy and the Spirit Most Holy, where man is crowned with the life that is God.

I, who was Francis of old who loved earth, sea and sky, remain your brother who hopes for the best in you all.

May I sign myself as of old, simply

Francis

10

To Educate the Heart

I am but a little child....
Give therefore thy servant
an understanding heart.

SOLOMON

The thought of possibility and of expansion should be guarded by the heart and mind of man. Those who have a tendency to accept negative concepts about themselves or their future again and again produce negative fruit on their tree of life. But the mind that has gleaned wisdom and accepted it will see the need to call forth from the very presence of life the God-given gift of its own reality.

The reality of unlimited possibility affords the individual a sense of hope. And the sense of hope brings confidence where the sense of struggle once reigned. One who truly hopes in God, his Mighty I AM Presence, replaces the sense of struggle with a newly found responsibility born of faith in his ultimate destiny.

Whereas karma, the law of the circle, returns to each one what he sends out, the control of karma is best established by an awareness of the best possibilities available in a given set of circumstances. Hence, the right kind of spiritual education is the determining factor in man's unfolding destiny.

Mere Tradition Is No Basis for Truth

In bygone years the word *claptrap* was applied to questionable and spurious teachings. Even today there is a trend toward lightly dismissing the unacclaimed sources of the best truths. In these days of travail when the darkness of educated ignorance covers the world, it is easy for men to look with misplaced faith to the old established orders whose only claim to integrity is often in their longevity. Yet time alone can never clothe ignorance in the vestments of truth.

We admit that some of the old orders have preserved the truth inviolate through the ages. A few have even added the progressive revelations of the Divine which have been vouchsafed by heaven.

Yet we would point out that in this age many leaders of the world's humanitarian and religious institutions have lost the first love of their founders. They have been turned away into the delusions of the world which are both anti-Christ and anti-God, hence anti-purpose and anti-spiritual. An evolutionary method that confines itself solely to the needs of social progress and that gauges its worth according to the shortsightedness of man's mortal span seldom contributes to the progressive reality of infinite man.

Darkness cannot produce light; neither can light produce darkness. For the nature of the one is the vibrant vitality of life, and the nature of the other is the somber shadow of nihilism.

Direct Apprehension of the Mind of God

Rejoice, then, for your salvation is at hand! It lies at the point where the educated consciousness contacts the mind of God. But an education that is derived solely from this world and is based upon the changing principles of man's understanding of the material universe can never hold an enduring promise before one's gaze. Nor will an education necessarily elevate consciousness.

We who are steadfast and unwavering in our search for eternal truth welcome you to examine the source of your knowledge and beliefs with a view to determining what is real and what is not real in your consciousness. For only by so doing will you recognize the reality that we shall unfold in concert with your Higher Self.

Those inner experiences that are the by-products of the soul's contact with universal truth will still the inharmonious voices of the world. And they will reveal the peace that can be obtained from communion with the divine intent.

Some do not understand that it is never enough for the Divine to intend or to plan man's destiny. Man must align himself with the divine intent through the consent of his will and his active implementation of that will.

Life Is Mastered Through the Spirit of God

If Cain had perceived the tenderness of the relationship between Abel and God, he could have established the same relationship between himself and God. He would not have murdered Abel, who had wed himself to the Christ. And like Abel, his sense of God's reality would have been exalted.

Cain's experience through the labyrinth of his human consciousness was an opportunity to exalt a sense of equality among brethren in the sight of God. But Cain's vision was not God's vision. Unlike Abel, he failed to accept his own divine estate.[1] Thus, as is often the case, the one to whom the opportunity was given chose to base his actions on a false sense of inferiority.

"Behold, I come quickly. Hold that fast which thou hast, that no man take thy crown."[2] This scriptural admonishment reveals the individual's sovereign need to guard his light. For principalities and powers of darkness ever attempt to despoil the nature of his being. In this wise, they would make him jealous of others and cause him to seethe with resentment and become a victim of self-inflicted wounds.

The key to the divine domain lies in each one's own Higher Self, not in that of others. Each emotional upheaval where the personality, through a warped sense of inferiority, lashes out at another part of life produces a karmic reaction which further delays that one's spiritual progress.

Jesus said, "Search the scriptures, for in them *ye think* ye have eternal life. And they are they which testify of me."[3] No man can inherit life or master it through a mere repetition of the divine letter of the Word. Life is mastered through the spirit of truth which was implanted in man from the very beginning. His turning away from that spirit, his turning away from the divine image to involvement in the sense of struggle (which makes the struggle) is the source of every untutored act.

Love, Wisdom and Power in Perfect Balance

True education is the education of the spirit. For it is through the spirit of God that the individual learns to govern himself through universal principle—by love, wisdom and power in perfect balance. Understanding the need to contribute to this universal triad, each individual must daily strive to understand the totality of his being and his relationship to the whole as well as to the parts.

When this is accomplished, the drawing rights of the individual upon the universal mind become a matter of record and of merit. As soon as the student realizes his place in the cosmic scheme, the Golden Rule becomes practical. He sees that it is futile to not be informed by reason and justice.

Malevolent forces have sought to involve man in such intricacies of thought and feeling as to conceal from his gaze the simplicity of reality and universal justice. Thus, in an unjust and an unreal world, Justice seems proverbially blind. But in reality she is not.

It is not God who must be corrected, but man who must be corrected by God. For we deal with the universal principle of the creative flame, the twin electromagnetic pulsation that draws into manifestation the designs of the mind of God in man.

Counterfeiters of Reality

The social diseases of the times are clearly displayed to all who would pause to consider the need for a purification of art forms. It is easy to see why art, music, sculpture, the theater and even language itself have been tampered with in this age. For they are the lever by which the consciousness of the youth and of the entire race can be and have been warped.

In reality, these are the instruments which God has designed to communicate to man the spirit of his wisdom. They are the media which are intended to convey the eternal verities of the mind of God to the spiritual senses of man. And they penetrate even the unawakened consciousness.

No wonder the counterfeiters of reality are busy twenty-four hours a day weaving a spell of nihilism into the fabric of culture! By contrast, we commend men to the simple joys of realization, not only through worship but also through application to the soundness of the laws of God which possess the power to educate the heart.

Drink of the Fount of Knowledge

One who possesses an educated heart will recognize that he must first assess his potential based upon his present record. Then he must take stock of his imagination (i.e., his ability to image forth reality). His imagination under the direction of God and the laws of divine justice can and should conceive a realistic goal that may be accomplished within one's life span.

Men should not ignore wisdom's laws. Those who drink of the fount of knowledge with pure motive, even in so-called old age, will draw to themselves a treasury of spiritual knowledge which they may use in the near or distant future. This is accomplished through the process of solar magnetism, which holds spiritual gifts within the orbit of the personal self.

Life is continual, and there is magic in believing and in hoping for a better tomorrow. But that magic must not be dissipated into channels of doubt and fear. It must not be allowed to dissolve in a gaze at yesteryear and its attendant failures. The being and consciousness of man must expand its own faith in universal purpose and draw upon a firsthand knowledge of the divine schemes rather than upon human ones.

Many forms of self-expression must be altered to conform to the divine ideal. Man must not only be willing to conform to the divine intent, but he must also be able to foster it. The heart that applies itself to the Creator's intent is the joyous heart that overcomes the world through the consciousness of the Christ.

Neither the momentums of self nor of others ought to be used as excuses for one's failures or as weights upon the soul. The soul must be free to drink of the fount of truth and to realize that behind the appearance world lies an infinite world of masterful causes, a treasure-house of the divine mind.

Let the self lay claim to these gifts and graces, that the self may muster the will, the wisdom and the wherewithal to overcome through light.

To the many valedictorians in our class I say, Victory!

Meru

11

Human Moods

Let nothing upset you, nothing frighten you.
Everything is changing; God alone is changeless.
Patience attains the goal. Who has God lacks
nothing; God alone fills all his needs.

TERESA OF AVILA

The swing of human moods is a predominant force by which the happiness and hopes of men are temporarily dashed upon the rocks. Thus, to understand and control the moods that seize one's consciousness is to understand and master the self in a most effective way.

First, let us show that the word *mood* is related to the word *moon* and that the lunar force that acts upon the tides also affects the feeling body of man and temporarily distorts his emotional nature. The interaction of people's emotional bodies in the ebb and flow of positive and negative polarities and in the juxtaposition of good and evil creates lunar fields within those who are involved with psychic energies. The effect of these forcefields on those who come within their orbit is similar to the effect of the moon in her cycles.

One of the problems involved with lunar influences is people's tendency to identify with their moods. Therefore, the student of the light must come apart from the world of moods. He must learn that by attuning his consciousness with the divine nature he can reverse the tide of his human moods and become the master rather than the slave of his feelings.

Cultivate a Sense of Detachment from Self

Unfortunately, those who practice self-analysis are often not objective when it comes to their own personalities. Even men of science—skilled in medicine and psychiatry as well as those who have been trained in psychology, philosophy and the physical and social sciences—are seldom able to solve their own problems. This is because they plunge headlong into a subjective sense of them, losing all perspective in matters in which they are emotionally involved.

Therefore, we advocate that you cultivate a deliberate sense of detachment from the self, especially during those crucial periods when you are compelled to ask yourself, "What is acting in my world?" When you can recognize any problem for what it is as though it were happening to someone else, you will find that it will have less hold upon you and you will be able to rise above the downward pull of moods.

Your Holy Christ Self and your beloved God Presence are eager for you to become the master of your world. For when you do, you will be able to see just what is acting when vicious forces, whether your own or another's, seek to subvert the spiritually progressive happiness that you desire to manifest.

Dare to Do God's Will

As we have said, the human personality restrains the course of the highest love as it meanders through the personal labyrinth where self-identification creates its own canyon walls. Yet the highest power is the highest power. And the highest love is the highest love. Both are able to overflow the banks of self-imposed limitation. This opens the way for the purifying energies of the Holy Spirit to inundate the soul.

People's tendency to identify with the lowest common denominator of human behavior should be recognized as contrary to divine principle. And it does not matter whether they identify with their own worst deeds or another's.

Therefore, to dare to do God's will must be the fervent cry of the man of the Spirit who would overcome all obstacles including self-woven shrouds of negation. Once and for all the soul cries out, "I want to be free!" But with each new challenge she is confronted with an impenetrable door whose mysterious face will not yield to the hungry and thirsty traveler.

Meekness Is Graciousness and Strength

Time waits for no man, for the vehicle of divine opportunity moves on. A balanced understanding of divine love, wisdom and power should be maintained during periods of personal struggle as well as in times of social upheaval. For then the fiery intensity of the cosmos is able to burn through the obstacles in self and society without scorching the evolving consciousness of men.

But this becomes true only when the disciple is able to stand aside and bow before his own Mighty I AM Presence. Carefully balanced on the razor's edge of pure reason, he is able, then, to keep the flame of life on behalf of many innocent souls.

He is in the world but not of the world. And from this vantage, he perceives the need to defend his cosmic rights against the forces which would defraud him and all mankind of their divine inheritance. He knows that the strength that is sufficient for the day will be forthcoming when he asks the assistance of heaven as a humble servant-son.

Man who dares to do the will of God ought not to dare without meekness. For the meek shall inherit the earth.[1] The type of meekness of which we speak is the quality of graciousness. It is manifest in those who know the source of their strength and use their knowledge not against other parts of life but for the emancipation of all.

Control Your Moods
Through Divine Understanding

I am well aware that all of these matters appear simple on the surface. And often individuals who read our instruction are so struck by its simplicity that they cry out, "But I already know that!" They almost resent our method of teaching by repetition.

But let me say again, it is not what you know that counts but what you do! And if you really have the knowledge of the Law, it will not be just an accretion of knowledge, a weighty tome of words partially retained in the brain and computerized for instant playback. It will be an active state of understanding.

"With all thy getting, get understanding."[2] For it is divine understanding that makes possible the individual unfoldment of divine power in the conscious will of man. Divine understanding alone assures man that he will be able to control and eventually free himself from destructive tendencies.

The doctrine of *ahimsa,* or harmlessness toward life, is truly an example of the effulgence of the Christ nature in manifestation. However, even as Archangel Michael and the Lord Jesus Christ did not hesitate in their contentions with evil to say, "Get thee behind me, Satan!"[3] so the student must not hesitate. When he realizes that he is being influenced by the phases of the moon—the new moon, the first quarter, the full moon and the third quarter—he should rebuke those lunar energies which are foreign to his true nature. He must, if he would be freeborn, always control his moods before they control him.

Detoxifying the Soul

Mood energies often penetrate between the sheaths of the four lower bodies. This creates great discomfort (both psychic and physical) because the nerves are temporarily polarized to the astral plane. To counter this influence, commit yourself to the Holy Spirit through devout prayer. Give dynamic decrees and call upon the violet transmuting flame to surround the four lower bodies. This will invariably spiritualize consciousness if the supplicant truly desires to be one with God.

Sometimes a change of pace is all that is necessary to

prevent the further encroachment of negative moods upon the psyche. Often the four lower bodies need time to recover from the influence of moods. For when you are overwhelmed by moods of anger, fear, grief, resentment or a general feeling of irritation, completely foreign psychic substance invades the soul. The soul must, therefore, be given time to throw off this substance just as the physical body must expel toxins.

Those who are subject to moods are frequently labeled "moody." Many are even proud of their moods, for they feel that in the name of freedom they have the right to express whatever they choose. But cosmic law proves otherwise. And whereas they certainly have the right to do as they will, the gift of free will is never abused with impunity.

Dominion over the Self

The ascended masters, the elder brothers of the race, always desire to bring the balance of the Christ to their students. For we know full well that all children of the light will one day find themselves at odds with the world. When that time comes, it is well to have developed a degree of mastery over one's energies that they be not lost in an unguarded moment.

We earnestly believe that the ability to control one's moods is vital to self-mastery. It will bring the individual closer to an understanding of and dominion over the self.

All too frequently, even students of the light think they can indulge themselves in moods or states of reverie simply because this is a habit they have learned to enjoy. Actually, this is a most dangerous indulgence, for the entertainment of moods can be confused with the creation of a spiritually receptive consciousness. Furthermore, prolonged involvement of the psyche in mood energies greatly diminishes one's faculties of Christ-discrimination.

We recommend that the student be receptive, that he wait upon the Lord and that he open his heart in what we might term "a receptive mood." In this frame of mind, he can be drawn into a higher spiritual state.

However, it should be borne in mind that human ideas are never enhanced by their circulation in the human consciousness. For an idea or a state of consciousness to change its polarity, it must be subjected to the higher will, to the higher love and to the higher intelligence of the mind of God.

Purify Your Mind with the Flames of God

Lingering residual magnetism in the subconscious regions of the mind can be purified and changed without ever surfacing to the conscious level. This is accomplished through the power of prayers and decrees as the supplicant invokes the violet transmuting flame. Those who have never experimented with the flames of God for the purposes of self-improvement and the raising of consciousness should not find fault with this method until they have experimented with it for at least six months.

Even then, if they would give their spiritual teachers at least half the chance which they expect life to give them, they should consider that perhaps their technique is undeveloped or their own density too great to yield in such a relatively short time. Therefore, they should continue to learn and use God's laws governing the scientific use of the flames—especially the violet flame.

Each day is an opportunity for the soul to attain an element of his eternal mastery. You do not pass in one moment from the human octave to the divine, but step by step you climb wisdom's golden stairs.

Study thyself to show thyself approved unto God.[4]

Devotedly, I remain

Lanto

12

Action and Reaction

Ali was quiet and then finally answered, . . .
"I have no longing except for the One. When a wind
of personal reaction comes, I do not go along with it.
There are many winds full of anger, and lust and
greed. They move the rubbish around, but the
solid mountain of our true nature stays
where it's always been."

RUMI

We must consider both the
diffusion of consciousness and its concentration. Ideal-
ists and spiritual seekers frequently dissipate their energies far and wide. Some people, on the other hand,
concentrate their attention so completely as to block
their receptivity to new ideas or to the free exchange of
concepts with others.

It is logical and sane to establish boundaries to one's
consciousness.[1] Otherwise, the weighty mental baggage

of erstwhile and tramp thoughts might easily break down the necessary framework required to maintain a functional field of action. Even so, one must be careful that these boundaries do not create excessive rigidity that inhibits receptivity

Soul Affinities

Quite frequently in examining an individual's akashic records, we find that souls are attracted to each other solely by their mutual karma. Yet one of the wisest masters of old, Sri Magra, once said, "Affinities are the 'fine ties' that are established in the perfect balance of the heart where the natural affections are enhanced by the feeling of delight in givingness as well as in a gracious state of receptivity."

Let souls be drawn together, then, according to their highest calling in God. Let magnanimous hearts unite in service. For their delight in the law of God can overcome the karmic conditions that would otherwise pit them against one another.

Miscommunication Causes Misunderstanding

The unfortunate state of the human ego in its sense of personal commitment to other egos often destroys beautiful friendships before they are born. We find this to be true whenever a breakdown in communication causes misunderstandings. While such misunderstandings are admittedly a farce (and no one should bear ill will toward another because of them), we often note the human tendency to mimic the worst examples in every age rather than the best.

The psalmist observed the senseless activities of the people and asked, "Why do the heathen rage and the people imagine a vain thing?"[2] And in reality, what can you do about it when people insist on having their own way?

The wayward child seldom realizes just why he acts as he does, nor does he know why the reactions of life (the return of karma) appear. We face, then, both action and reaction. In the course of a day's events, human beings continually make things happen unless in their overbearing neutrality they are blown about by every wind.

Overcome the Habit of Reaction

The eternal God desires to help the advanced disciple understand that if he is to be a part of the prime mover of the universe, a part of the Holy Spirit, he must keep the way of wholeness in the whole body of God insofar as he is able. This means that he must not react to the actions of others.

From the Dhammapada, the teachings of the Buddha ring clear concerning the wailing of men: "'He abused me, he beat me, he defeated me, he robbed me'—in those who harbor such thoughts hatred will never cease."[3] Down through the ages, men have recited their grievances against other parts of life. We doubt not that many of these grievances have been based on injustices, but we believe that happiness is most important. As the Buddha said, "If a man speaks or acts with a pure thought, happiness follows him, like a shadow that never leaves him."[4]

When one allows oneself to constantly suffer as the victim of someone else's actions, it is often because his own reactions have set up reactions in others. When one becomes accustomed to a climate of domination— imposing himself upon others and in turn being imposed upon by others—he knows not his own freedom nor is he able to impart freedom to others.

Therefore, the greatest step the disciple can take is to stop reacting to the perceived mistakes of others. It is enough that an individual has erred, but when you add your own error to his you have "a compound fracture." Usually these situations are not easily mended. The more sensitive souls among mankind often revolve the chastisement of another's ill-chosen remarks or, in some cases, well-chosen remarks which were misinterpreted.

Living Midst Disturbing Conditions

The business of living requires exquisite care. If one is to be mindful of the self while being mindful of others, he must hold dear the virtue of perfect balance at all times, especially in the midst of disturbing conditions. Rudyard Kipling phrased it well: "If you can keep your head when all about you / Are losing theirs and blaming it on you.... / Yours is the Earth and everything that's in it."[5]

As Lanto explained in the previous chapter, the influence of the moon plays a part in disturbing situations. Its pull is often greatest upon those who refuse to acknowledge it. Many draw lunar vibrations to themselves through their impure feelings, which polarize them to the astral plane. This accumulation of negative energy can cause a fragile peace to be easily shattered by trivia. If you can "keep your head," you can further the divine plan for others by guarding against accumulating undesirable records in your own book of life.

How fortunate it is that we can impart to you this understanding. How fortunate it is that we are able to reach through the veil as we do here. We counsel you from our level both simply and profoundly to help you understand and rule yourself.

Gilding the Lily from Without

You would be surprised, I am certain, if you could see the records of the billions of lifestreams evolving upon earth, to note how many truly delightful people allow themselves to be harried by their own careless and vain expressions. And if they were honest and you were to ask them what they get out of life during periods of stress, they would probably answer, "Nothing."

But we would disagree. For what they get out of it, in reality, is misqualified energy which places a weight on the balance of life. This counteracts what virtue they have expressed and should continue to express in their lives. The man who is careless with his energy places in jeopardy not only the present in which he lives but also the future in which he hopes to live.

Men cry out that they wish to please God. They beat upon their breasts, and they vow with fierce determination that they will never again depart from the law of their being. Yet the record is clear: old and crusty momentums often draw more of their kind to your world. They pull down the otherwise buoyant craft of self into the rapids of life where experiences blend into a montage of whirling energy, a movement too fast to stabilize.

Then, in a state of desperation, men turn to undesirable panaceas. These may include dangerous drugs, sexual indulgences, the use of intoxicants, a display of violence or an exhibition of the ego calculated to win admiration.

This is truly gilding the lily from without. And it not

only spoils the natural beauty of the flower, but it also ties up energy. If this energy were permitted to flow from within, it would naturally open the bud of self into such octaves of beauty and supremacy as to stimulate the most noble expression in all who would so order their lives.

Act on Inspiration from God

We direct you to thoughtfully consider the dangers of reaction. The only safe reaction to external affairs is to act on inspiration from on high and from within.

Respond with joy to the positive energies flowing into your world from the fount of truth. Cooperating with life's energies will eventually replace reactions to negative stimuli which produce fiery and useless battles.

We hold before the vision of the ascending son a burst of renewed hope. Progress is best made by stopping the expansion of error and by turning all energy into one wide channel of glorious spiritual achievement. This practice will enhance godly development and supply your every need.

May we say together, "Fortunately, I AM!"

Kuthumi

13

The Hidden Man of the Heart

In the center of the castle of Brahman,
our own body, there is a small shrine in the form
of a lotus-flower, and within can be found a small
space. We should find who dwells there,
and we should want to know him.

CHANDOGYA UPANISHAD

Let us open the understanding to the doorway of Self. Self is not the image that appears, that seems to be but is naught, that masquerades behind the persona. Self is not the mask, nor is it the karmic record that is filled with undesirable qualities which man repudiates in his heart.

In the struggle between good and evil, negative forces would hide man's real image and glorify his pseudoimage. This they do to control men by warping their motives and surrounding them with fear. But the key to escape is simple. If you will remain steadfast in a childlike sense of wonder and trust in God, we can this day dispel all doubt and fear from your consciousness, regardless of your intellectual level.

First you must understand that the image that appears is not real. Second, the image that does not readily appear but that *is* real is often hidden. And third, this hidden image is the image that God did make and that he saw was good.[1]

God's Law Raises You to Greater Glory

Subtle forces of the serpent mind roam the planet. This they do through a fraudulent theology and a psychopolitical treachery resulting in an invasion of men's minds. Meanwhile, they spawn obsessions which continue to downgrade the human race by amplifying supposed or actual errors. They try to hide the beautiful image of God in which each of his offspring were made.

We would restore your sense of dignity and self-worth that we might help you to understand yourself. It is not that we would say the evil that men have done is no cause for punishment, for the Word of God is clearly stated: "Be not deceived; God is not mocked. For whatsoever a man soweth, that shall he also reap. For he that soweth to his flesh shall of the flesh reap corruption, but he that soweth to the Spirit shall of the Spirit reap life everlasting."[2]

But this law was written for positive reasons. When God said you will reap what you sow, he referred to the law of givingness and service whereby a star of minute proportions could attain to a greater glory. Permit a greater measure of the glory of God to flow through your consciousness, for this is the only means whereby the gifts of the eternal kingdom may be permanently retained.

The world is full of condemnation. Mankind do not understand that when they condemn one another they also condemn themselves. Nor do they understand that condemnation is a tangible misqualification of God's energy. They also fail to realize that when they laugh at one another they are actually laughing in the dark at God, who is in the light. For God dwells in the inner light of every man.[3]

Those who speak against the veiled prophet who abides within as the hidden man of the heart[4] speak out of the darkness of themselves against the light. That they know it not and are ignorant is no excuse.

Your Divine Origin

In teaching you to understand yourself, we must remove from your eyes the scales of injustice that have traduced your immortal reality.

You are a child of the light,
You were created in the image divine,
You are a child of infinity,
You dwell in the veils of time,
You *are* a son of the Most High!

To ray your light and to serve
Is to do the will divine,
By being the living Word.
No darkness can long endure
Before the radiant light.
The truth will make you secure
And ready your soul for flight—
The ascension is the goal.
As Jesus rose from the sod,
He inspired man to enfold
Himself in the mantle of God.

I AM is the name of the Father,
I AM is the name of the Son,
I AM is the Spirit Most Holy—
Ye all are clothed by the One.

He will guide and guard you forever,
He will carry you far in his arm,
He hides himself from the clever,
He enshrines the poor with his charm.

God lives in your soul, the image of Self—
To know it will change your view.
God lives in the light that shines from within,
He breaks his bread with the few.

He hears our calls and answers,
His love is the light of men.
Accept, then, his understanding—
Your wonderful way to win.

I AM is the name you must call on—
'Tis being so broad and true.
For the narrow confinements of selfhood
Can only hide from view

The face of forever in heaven
Unfolding within the soul.
His bread is the precious leaven
To raise us all to our goal.

You Build for Eternity

Won't you understand, then, that as your Real Self
has no part in karmic records, in personality traits, in
the sense of struggle and separation, so you must be
alive forevermore. As Jesus said to John on Patmos,
"Behold, I am alive forevermore... and have the keys of
hell and of death,"[5] so the development of the deathless

consciousness of your Creator will enable you to build for eternity.

The work you do is not for a moment. It is not for a family you will lose or who will lose you. It is not for a course that will be won or for a diploma earned. These are pinnacles in time. These are but passing landmarks on the road to an ever-transcending reality, for the work of the Father and of the Father through the Son is for eternity.

Understand thy Highest Self, then, as the God of very gods. As you face this concept, the lower self falls upon its knees. As the Christ, the eternal Mediator, bows to the Father, good becomes All-in-all. Man enters the sudden stream of overcoming self-realization.

He fears no loss, for he sees that the blackened image of the synthetic self that has sought to cast down his immortal birthright is not real! Therefore, he quickly replaces it with the divine image and humbly holds himself in the consciousness of the son who awaits his divine inheritance.

Your Living Identity Is the Eternal God

These simple phrases, meditated upon again and again, will reestablish the currents of the ascension flame within the fabric of the soul. These gentle graces, thought upon with utter devotion, will take the sting out of the battle of life. They will balance the service of the man of great spiritual attainment with that of the man who is just beginning.

As it was spoken long ago, "But many that are first shall be last; and the last first."[6] Until men merge with their divine image and with their divine inheritance, they should not consider who is free from karma and who is not, who has more karma and who has less karma. For the way of overcoming is strictly a matter of consciously realizing that one's living identity is the deathless, birthless, eternal God.

Through identification with this eternal God, the lodestone of the Presence becomes the magnet that focuses energy and purpose in the individual monad, drawing him ever upward in the great sounding stream of universal progress. A god is born. "Ye must be born again."[7] No longer wedded to the changing, shifting sands of personality, of frustration and of struggle, man understands himself as one with his own beloved I AM Presence.

The Presence of All Life Is One

But a note of caution must be sounded here. No one must use his Divine Presence as a cudgel to harm others upon the Path. No one must say, "My Presence is over your Presence." For the Presence of all life is one. The delicate interaction between the souls of men that is a development of the power and wisdom of the Presence always exudes the perfect activity of divine love.

The individual seeker on the Path would do well to understand clearly that he must put an end to the sense of struggle between himself and differing ideologies, concepts and personality traits of others. This does not require you to become aloof from humanity. Nor do we suggest that you fail to consider the statements of others politely and sincerely even though they may be functioning on the Path below the level of the Divine. We recommend instead that you establish your relationship with others on the basis of your relationship with your Holy Christ Self.

Let none construe our remarks to mean that you should presume to judge or to condemn other men, for your judgment rests with the Eternal. Your faith rests with God. Your hope rests with your future.

Give Your Life to God and Be Free

When you commend your life and your thoughts unto God, you automatically free the lower self from converging and diverging lines of karmic force. You draw into your unascended consciousness the beautiful qualities of the Presence that fulfill the necessary and lawful requirements that lead to your ultimate freedom in the light.

Oh, if only the students would grasp this principle! And then if they would reread this book until they have made it a part of the inner instruction that is written in the heart, they would find it much easier to manifest the freedom of genuine happiness in fulfilling their divine plan.

Lovingly, in the light of daily progress, moving onward to perfection, I remain

Meru

14

The Memory of the Soul

Where is truth but in the soul itself?

HYPATIA

Not words, words, words but the Word. "In the beginning was the Word."[1] In the middle are words, words, words. But in the ending only the Word will remain.

The students who would understand themselves should realize that the expansion of the middle—a term which I use symbolically to describe the finite realm—is intentional in order to provide in the field of *kal* (time) and *dèsa* (space) what may be called a fort of opportunity. Here the chaff of human experience can be separated from the wheat of spiritual growth.[2] Here the false starts and the false moves that inscribed the karmic record upon the soul can be adjudicated and balanced. And here the beauty of realigning the consciousness and of manifesting the original purpose for which the individual took embodiment can best be served.

Fulfilling Earthly Responsibilities

Though it may be trite, we would say, "There is a way which seemeth right unto a man, but the end thereof are the ways of death."[3] The ways of death refer to the death of the human person, the stamping of "finis" on the dossier of an individual life.

Now, those who identify solely with personality expressions do actually die when the life energy that beats their hearts is withdrawn, for their existence was based entirely on the flesh. But some have already cast their anchors beyond the veil. They have relinquished their ties to the human person while simultaneously fulfilling their responsibilities and obligations in the world of form. These live on in the consciousness of immortality.

We would impart holy wisdom to men and women on the spiritual path. We would open the way for those who are in a state of becoming all that their I AM Presence would have them become. We say it is essential that before they exit the world they do not prematurely forsake the natural and reasonable obligations which they have made.

Care is a quality of the Deity. Therefore, God's

consideration for humanity prompts men to underwrite humanitarian endeavors while they are on earth and even beyond. These are the marks of God's own cosmic care and consideration for each one.

Reembodiment Provides the Opportunity to Attain Immortality

Reembodiment is the eternal God's sweeping program to give to humanity the fruits of the kingdom of the Spirit. It provides a renewal of opportunity to those who fail to make the grade in the first, second, third or subsequent battle for attainment.

To those who are not on the Path it provides a hopeful continuity. Thus, one day they might recognize the splendid purposes of life. Thereby they may become a part of the vanguard of the kingdom of angels, elementals and men who always seek to increase beauty in life everywhere.

Men can willingly surrender their habitual sense of identification with the changing, death-centered mortal personality. And at that moment they actually attain immortality. This act of surrender is a splendid one. It is truly a rebirth by the power of the Holy Spirit. It is a transfer of the consciousness from the forcefield of mortality, with its attendant sense of struggle, to the domain of the Holy Spirit—right while the individual consciousness occupies a physical body.

When this transfer occurs, the body need no longer be a liability to the soul. For the body itself can provide the necessary adjunct that will assist the soul in bringing about the ascension. This process culminates in the reunion of one's four lower bodies with the heart of his Divine Presence.

The I AM Presence is birthless and deathless. It holds contact with every part of life stretching to infinity. Thus, at the moment of awakening, the whole universe bursts into view within one's consciousness.

The Infinite Power of Prayer

Now let us understand clearly that we are talking about two forms of consciousness: (1) the consciousness of the outer self with its awareness of externals and (2) the consciousness of the soul with its inner knowing. The eyes of the soul once opened are able to witness the birth of star systems that even the most powerful telescopes cannot reach. They are able to respond to the prayer of a child suffering hardship with the divine pathos and the divine answer.

You can never truly serve the needs of all whom you love until you hold within your grasp the infinite power of God. We have witnessed healings upon earth that have been accomplished through the agency of embodied men and women who have made intercession for those in need.

Consider, then, what it means to be able to hold in your hands the globe of compassion as the scepter of power. You can assist, as God assists, in the development of the universe. You can be free from mortal limitation and commune with the immortals in their exalted state of consciousness. For they formerly passed through the same doorway which you will now be passing through as your soul awakens.

Awaken Your Soul's Memory

Dear ones, some of you may have difficulty in accepting the truth of reembodiment because you do not in your outer mind recall events of your past lives. Yet it is the soul's memory that is able to integrate all experience into a comprehensive whole.

The objective consciousness is naturally confined to the memory of the events of your present life. This persists until you learn to reach into the memory of the soul and draw forth with crystal clarity the patterns of life that integrate the allness of self into the allness of the universe. When this is done, it will not decrease happiness but tremendously increase it because a natural unfoldment of the divine memory will emerge from within.

Those who attempt to force these spiritual experiences with dangerous drugs or mental probings and exercises literally tear open the petals of the flower of the soul from the budding center. One day they will find the fallen petals at their feet, faded and dry, returning to the dust from which all things were made.[4] Only by recognizing that the soul within, the living soul that God made, possesses the capacity to span the centuries will you be able to enter into immortal life.

The soul has been neglected; the soul must be awakened. And man, too, must awaken himself to the soul's conscious awareness. He must never permit the desecration of the beautiful soul which the LORD God made in his own image.[5] The restoration of the son to the image of the Father is the precious way of salvation. And it is your own living Christ Self who wields this power of self-elevation.

See God as He Is

When every eye shall see him as he is,[6] they shall place their fingers upon the body of his substance. They shall feel the symmetry of the Spirit that is within him. They shall feel the electronic throb of his heartbeat. And the essence of his life will pour through the gar-ment he wears and flood their souls with identification with higher realms. Then shall man truly come to know who and what he is.

Man is God in the becoming, but he can never know this while he thinks earthly thoughts. He can never know this by worldly knowledge, for the things of this world are foolishness with God.[7] And in the eyes of God, the only real values are those that free man from the eclipse of being that has concealed the sun of God's Presence from his eyes. And it is this sun that will awaken his spiritual senses that enable him to see with Saint Paul the face of the Master and to hear his cry "It is hard for thee to kick against the pricks."[8]

"God loveth a cheerful giver"[9] and those who surrender sweetly, joyously to his program of hope for them and for the whole world are forerunners who understand the great, blazing noontide reality of themselves. These not only will to be free, but they will also *be* free.

Graciously, in the never-failing light of God, I remain

Lanto

15

The Consciousness of the Living God

Honor the highest thing in the
Universe; it is the power on which all
things depend; it is the light by which all
of life is guided. Honor the highest within
yourself; for it too is the power on which
all things depend, and the light by
which all life is guided.

MARCUS AURELIUS

I recently spoke to the disciples gathered at The Summit Lighthouse headquarters and I said, "Understand that the noontide is not the even and that the midnight hour is not the dawn." With this thought in mind, I would draw to a close my contribution to our training on understanding yourself, for there is a tendency on the part of humanity to regard themselves fixed in whatever state they find themselves at a given moment. It is almost as though they considered themselves to be that moment rather than the 'all-moment'.

The Word went forth of old: "With his stripes we are healed."[1] And the Word went forth again: "Their sins and iniquities will I remember no more."[2] Many grasped this principle with faint hope and others with fervent hope, but all desired their freedom from past responsibilities.

I have learned to trust God completely, for he is able to save to the uttermost those who believe on him.[3] But the faith that men have is but a goad to the works they must do. For through their works they must transpose the self from its habitual human affinity to an understanding of its eternal divine reality.

Come Apart from the World of Opposites

Therefore, you must not live in the sense of your present order or disorder, progress or struggle, fears or hopes. But you must come apart from all that makes up the world of opposites. For therein man alternates between his midnight and his noonday hour. Therein shades of expression pass from exaltation to depression and then back again to exaltation.

To dwell in the consciousness of the living God is to hold oneself in a state of such constant beauty as defies description in ordinary words. Only the tongues of angels could begin to describe what it is really like to dwell in realms of light.

Therein souls have the vast power-flow of eternity resident within. They have access to the great libraries of heaven with all of the considerations and works of the sons of God recorded there. They are able to glean therefrom the fruit of a continually self-renewing knowledge and to know that God's laws are divine coordinates. These coordinates are fixed as stars in the firmament— blazing points of light that will gladden the eyes of each little child who shall come to the knowledge of himself.

God's Laws Are Polestars to Guide You

So tender and so beautiful is the face of the Eternal One that those who are made in his similitude, those who occupy all of the vast planes of being, never cease to marvel at the great unity that is manifest in the diversity of heaven.

It is easy to see how earth's environmental influences can erode the fine substances of the soul. So it is easy to see how those who have attained to the higher consciousness of the angels and spiritual beings will have blotted from their minds all of the sense of struggle and pain that has been attendant with them throughout the span of their earthly lives.

The pleasures and displeasures that come to mankind—holding him now in the hot water of fear and then in the cool water of hope—are a source of continual pressure and pain. But he who delights in the law of God[4] and in the power of God's mind is content to convey to all generations the laws of the many mansions of the Father.[5] For these gleam in the heavens and bespeak promise to the souls of men. In a very real sense, the higher laws and the higher virtues are polestars to guide the mariners in this world toward their eternal realities.

The Home of Heaven Lives Within You

It is quite natural that men should fear to die. But some of you may be startled when I say that the soul has a greater fear of being born into the world of form than it does of leaving it.

The lower astral planes of life contain frightening and gruesome figures which seek to harm the soul as it journeys from one plane of existence to the next. But he who places his trust in God is able to draw the power of the angels and of the archangels to his defense and to rise out of those dense spheres and controlled realms. Then at last, the soul knows and it is known in the limitless and airy habitations of the planetary orbs, in interstellar space and even in the space within the self— its own "forty acres."

You sometimes think and speak of heaven as home, but you live as though earth were forever your dwelling place. When the home of heaven lives within you, the dwelling place of man is no longer important. For you can command the elements around you to be free. You can take dominion over environmental forces. And you can create through beauty and art a place which God himself will call home.

Through the span of the ages, men have changed the environments of their thoughts, their reading material and the images upon which they gaze. By cooperating with your I AM Presence to surround yourself with the kingdom of heaven, you will help to evolve the kingdom of God within you.

As you evolve these higher thoughts, bear well in mind that your self is also your neighbor's self. The good that flowers within you is also available to him, even as the flowers of his garden are available to you.

Internalize the Power of Your Spiritual Reality

Some may smile in the coarseness of their sensuality at these finer gestures of the angels which I am making. But I am confident that after reading the final chapter by beloved Meru, you will rejoice that you have had the opportunity to progress through its pages. And hopefully you will have progressed through the consciousness of

God's own understanding of himself which we have sought to convey.

Although man may be born in faint hope, he lives to see the day when that hope becomes the vital faith that carries him through all of the vicissitudes of life. I hope, then, for you, as does every son of heaven, that as you read and reread our offering, you will be able to internalize the glowing power of your spiritual reality.

This is truly a tangible manifestation that exists within the field of your consciousness. Cast aside pettiness and conditions that have hindered you from moving forward in your life, especially those that you have blown up out of all proportion.

I call to God for renewed perspective for each one of you, that you may vent your consciousness by opening the windows of the soul and by calling for the sunlight of his radiance to pour through. Our words may not always be new, but the consciousness Christ brings is ever new. The ideas that he will bring and the ideas that we will bring in his name will be not only new but also renewing. And one day we will clasp hands even as now in spirit and in essence we can clasp hearts.

As Saint Francis of old, I carried many hefty stones and threw them into place, even with my knee. Now I place my knees upon the eternal rock of the living Christ,[6] who is our joint salvation. And I pray with thee that the mantle of his peace may sustain thy heart at every moment—at the dawn producing hope and at the midnight hour producing an awareness of the coming dawn.

Your sincere friend of the ages,

Kuthumi

16

Taking Dominion over the Self

Not in the clamour of the crowded street,
Not in the shouts and plaudits of the throng,
But in ourselves, are triumph and defeat.

HENRY WADSWORTH LONGFELLOW

We have sought to cast upon the self what can be called the golden flame of precise illumination. If we have revealed a page, volumes remain to be written and read. Nevertheless, a helpful summation of what has been given is in order.

Man's delight in the inward laws of his own being will increase in majesty and in power through his realization that the gift of dominion lies within his own hand. Many wait for external conditions to shape their lives, and we acknowledge that to a great extent outer circumstances do control the lives of men.

But men must recognize that the inward affinities of the soul and the accumulations of good and bad karma are the promoters of their destiny. Therefore, to understand the inner man is essential to taking dominion over the earth.

God Dominion Is Not Mortal Domination

Taking dominion over one's world as God intends does not include the exerting of mortal control over others. Nor does it imply that individuals should be moved by every whimsy of mortal thought and feeling. But far too many among the children of God upon earth are unknowingly subject to control by others whose ideals and purposes are not part of the divine plan but are part of their own plan for personal domination.

Dominion and domination are not the same thing. To take dominion means to be aware of the cosmic potential that has been implanted within the self as a gift of the living God. Then one begins to externalize in the outer world of form the beautiful pattern which God holds for every man. On the other hand, the domination of mankind is the usurpation of his free will.

Impure Consciousness Muddies the Divine Plan

One of man's greatest mistakes is to fail to externalize the plan of God first in the inner world of the mind and then in the outer world of manifestation. For the divine plan is intimately involved with the subtleties of the inner radiance of the inner man of the heart. When that plan is passed through the muddied stream of the subconscious mind, filled as it is with its hodgepodge of vain imaginations, it is temporarily lost to the outer mind, which can then bring forth only the bane of ignorance upon the screen of life.

The purification of one's consciousness, then, is a vital prerequisite for the beginning student as well as for the more advanced along the Path who would truly find their way godward. The winged God Self cannot fly when its wings are clipped by human vanities or man's self-imposed limitations.

Man is truly a God in exile, but he need not remain so. He can purify his world through application to the heart of God, and he can invoke those cosmic flame patterns which are manifestations of the flow of the Christ consciousness.

It is the sense of sin as well as the involvement in iniquity that has promoted feelings of guilt. These cause men to go deeper and deeper into debt simply because they do not pay the debts they have already incurred.

Far too many among the children of earth seeking the light fail to understand that they themselves have created a pile of rubble. Moreover, they do not know that they can never complete the beautiful work of soul development until they have also engaged their energies in the process of self-purification.

The question has been raised: Shall a man purify and develop his soul simultaneously or must he complete his purification before he begins his development?

Beloved ones, let us put first things first. Purification is development, for even in the building of a house you must first clear the land and prepare the site before you can lay a proper foundation.

Effective Application of Spiritual Teachings

One of the problems that often confronts the more advanced students results from studying a great deal of spiritual law. They have often studied with a number of teachers and organizations who have taught partial yet effective truths. At certain points along the way, these students feel compelled to cast aside all that they have learned in order to grasp the eternal symbol of progression.

Let them learn that although names may vary, processes remain the same. We acknowledge that the techniques that are recommended for their spiritualization may differ according to the teacher. But the individual should always remember that his relationship to his God Presence remains the same.

Therefore, upon the student rests the responsibility of drawing from the teachings the effective application that will enable him to profit the most from the instruction. We do not exonerate the teacher of the responsibility of presenting the teaching in the best way possible. But what is the best way possible when one deals with minds in various states of progress, stemming from various beginnings?

Hindered by semantics, some become hopelessly lost and they eventually abandon their search for truth. This is unnecessary, for even the most advanced student does not hinder his progress by reexamining the basic principles of the Law as a point of review. Simply because you have already mastered a language skill does not mean that you cannot profit from a review of your earliest books or from an encounter with phrases now forgotten.

Such review will often revitalize the whole imaginative process and enable you to capture an inner picture of a host of subjects. When these are integrated into your being, they will add to your compendium of knowledge that is so valuable in the business of living.

Divine arts are no different from human ones. And we choose to think that the business of living is really a divine art, but far too many among mankind take this business for granted.

Your Christ Self Is the Orifice of Life

Long ago, one of the great followers of the Christ said: "Know ye not that your body is the temple of the Holy Ghost which is in you, which ye have of God, and ye are not your own? For ye are bought with a price: therefore glorify God in your body and in your spirit, which are God's."[1]

The descent of God into form was an opportunity for the personality (the form consciousness) through the nature of God individualized to attain to the completeness of the Godhead. The Christ is the cornerstone of the temple,[2] and your own Holy Christ Self is the mighty orifice of the fountain of life. As this opening is enlarged through your attunement with the Cosmic Christ and the expansion of your own level of awareness, the unfolding realities of your Divine Self will bring the peace that comes with a more comprehensive knowledge of the Law.

In our releases to mankind, both in our worded instruction and in the gentle radiation of our love that can be felt through the very pages themselves, we desire to bring you into the great sheepfold of the eternal Good Shepherd. The bishop of your soul is the living Christ within you. And unless you maintain contact with this mighty universal being, you will never come up out of the human consciousness.

Your Christ Self is charged with seeing to it that you become the fullness of all that God is. For thereby you will fulfill your destiny and return to the divine image. He is the door, and all who climb up another way are thieves and robbers.[3]

Christ is the light of the world.[4] But centuries ago the children who had only a partial glimpse of reality twisted and warped the great Christic truths that would have given all men their freedom long ago. Therefore, we ask you today in the holy name of your God Presence to realize that your Higher Self is very much involved in the business of living and so must your lower self be.

Be a Beacon of Hope to Others

Entirely too many among mankind function mechanically, repeating with cyclic regularity their boring routines without ever realizing their opportunity to bring the Christ light into the simplest and humblest task. Whatever you do can contribute not only to the development of yourself and to your daily understanding of your Higher Self, but it can also provide a beacon of hope to others with whom you may be associated.

The grace that is not too proud to become as a little child in spiritual things,[5] to stoop that it might enter the narrow, sometimes low doorway of events, will ultimately find itself at the feet of infinite grace. Surely one day the dawn of your Higher Self will become the noontide, and the fulfillment of the cycles of being will signify a return to the Father's reality.

The flame of my etheric retreat over Lake Titicaca rises high. May all aspire to the highest illumination of the Real Self.

I remain devoted to your light,

Meru

Man, Know Thy Self…
as God

THE CHART OF YOUR DIVINE SELF

Your Divine Self

Behold the Creator of the world, all of him,
within myself. . . . He is in my heart, he is in heaven:
Both there and here he shows himself to me
with equal glory.

SYMEON THE NEW THEOLOGIAN

You have a unique spiritual destiny. One of the keys to fulfilling that destiny is knowing that you have a divine nature and that you have a direct relationship to God. To help you understand this relationship, the ascended masters have designed the Chart of Your Divine Self.

This Chart is a portrait of you and of the God within you. It is a diagram of you and your potential to become who you really are. The Chart of Your Divine Self depicts three levels of your inner reality, corresponding to the Three Persons of the Trinity and the Divine Mother.

The Personal Presence of God—
Your I AM Presence

The upper figure is your I AM Presence and corresponds to the First Person of the Trinity—the Father, who is one with the Mother. The I AM Presence is the absolute perfection of your divine reality. It is the spirit of the living God who is individualized in each one of us. It is your personalized "I AM THAT I AM," which is the name of God that he revealed to Moses on Mount Sinai.

According to the level of your devotion, your I AM Presence may be very near or very far from you. "Draw nigh to God," counsels the Epistle of James, "and he will draw nigh to you."[1] When you draw near to God through loving thoughts, feelings and actions, your I AM Presence will draw near to you, enfolding you in his love. But when you engage in unloving thoughts, feelings and actions, you automatically repel your I AM Presence.

Your I AM Presence is surrounded by seven concentric spheres. These pulsating spheres of spiritual energy make up your Causal Body. They contain the record of the good works you have performed to the glory of God and the blessing of your fellowman since your very first incarnation on earth.

Whenever you do something for the sake of serving God and man—and not for self-gain—the positive energy of your good works ascends to your Causal Body and increases its size. Your Causal Body is like a cosmic bank where you lay up for yourself "treasures in heaven."[2] When you need more energy to accomplish more good works, you can ask your I AM Presence to draw from the reserves stored in your Causal Body and to supply you with the extra impetus you need.

Each sphere of the Causal Body is a different color, denoting one of the "seven rays." Rays are frequencies of light, and each ray is associated with a different attribute or aspect of God's consciousness. The colors and corresponding qualities of the spheres, from the center of the Causal Body to the periphery, are:

1. White sphere: purity, discipline and joy
2. Yellow sphere: wisdom, understanding, enlightenment and illumination
3. Pink sphere: compassion, kindness, charity, love and beauty
4. Violet sphere: mercy, forgiveness, justice, freedom and transmutation
5. Purple-and-gold sphere: service, ministration, peace and brotherhood
6. Green sphere: truth, science, healing, abundance, vision and music
7. Blue sphere: faith, will, power, perfection and protection

Your Inner Teacher—
The Holy Christ Self

The middle figure in the Chart of Your Divine Self represents the Holy Christ Self. You can think of your Holy Christ Self as your chief guardian angel and dearest friend. He is your inner teacher, who inspires you to take responsible and assertive action on behalf of those in need. Just as the I AM Presence is the Universal Presence of God individualized for each of us, so the Holy Christ Self is the Universal Christ Presence individualized for each of us.

In truth, there is but one LORD and one God. Therefore Moses said, "Hear, O Israel, the LORD our God is one LORD."[3] Yet God, out of the depths of his love for us, gave every one of us an image of himself, a "photograph" if you will. For he desired that we should not forget him during our long sojourn on earth. This divine image of God that is your very own is your individual I AM Presence.

It is as if a photograph of God were published in a magazine. Ten million copies of that photograph do not add up to ten million Gods, but only one. Likewise, there is but one Son of God, who is the one Universal Christ. Yet God, in his infinite mercy, gave you and me an exact replica of the original—our Holy Christ Self.

The Holy Christ Self corresponds to the Second Person of the Trinity—the Son of the Father-Mother God. The Bible refers to Jesus Christ as the "Son of God" because Jesus had become one with his Holy Christ Self. In fact, both the Father (the I AM Presence) and the Son (the Holy Christ Self) dwelt fully in Jesus, as Paul testified when he said, "In him [Jesus] dwelleth all the fullness of the Godhead bodily."[4]

The Path of Personal Christhood

Jesus came to the fore in the two-thousand-year period known as the Piscean age because God chose him to be the archetypal Christ, or avatar, of that age. That means that for the past two thousand years, Jesus has served as the representative of and the embodiment of the Universal Christ, the Son of God.

Jesus' mission was to demonstrate to every soul on earth how to reunite with the Holy Christ Self. Jesus was the example of what we can become. He wanted all of us to walk our *own* path of personal Christhood.

We can make rapid progress on our path of personal Christhood by imitating Jesus Christ or any of the ascended masters. The ascended masters are the saints and adepts of East and West who walked their own path of personal Christhood, became one with their Christ Self, fulfilled their reason for being and are now reunited with God. As you live in imitation of Jesus and the ascended masters, day by day your Holy Christ Self descends closer and closer to you. You and your Holy Christ Self become one.

In the Chart of Your Divine Self, the descending dove of the Holy Spirit is depicted just above the Holy Christ Self.

Your Divine Spark—The Threefold Flame

The shaft of white light descending from the I AM Presence through the Holy Christ Self to the lower figure in the Chart is the crystal cord. It is the "umbilical cord," the lifeline, that ties you to your I AM Presence. Ecclesiastes referred to it as the silver cord.[5] Through this cord God's light, life and consciousness flow to you perpetually, empowering you to think, feel, reason and experience the wonders of life from your first breath to your last.

Your crystal cord also nourishes the threefold flame that is ensconced in the secret chamber of your heart. The threefold flame, also called the divine spark, is literally a spark of sacred fire that God has transmitted from his heart to yours.

The mystics of the world's religions have contacted the divine spark, describing it as the seed of divinity within. Buddhists, for instance, speak of the "germ of

Buddhahood"[6] that exists in every living being. In the Hindu tradition, the Katha Upanishad speaks of the "light of the Spirit" that is concealed in the "secret high place of the heart" of all beings. It describes this Spirit as "smaller than the smallest atom, greater than the vast spaces."[7]

The divine spark, the threefold flame, has three "plumes." These plumes embody the three primary attributes of God—power, wisdom and love—and correspond to the Trinity of Father, Son and Holy Spirit. The white-fire core from which the threefold flame springs corresponds to God the Mother. By accessing the power, wisdom and love of God anchored in your threefold flame, you can fulfill your reason for being.

As you commune with God and pray to him, you can visualize your threefold flame burning in the secret chamber of your heart. You have a blue plume on your left, a yellow plume in the center and a pink plume on your right.

The blue plume (corresponding to God the Father) is the anchor point within you for the power and will of God. It sparks your willpower, your faith and your determination to fulfill your life's mission. The yellow plume (corresponding to God the Son) anchors within you the discriminating intelligence of the mind of God and his wisdom. The pink plume (corresponding to God the Holy Spirit) anchors the love, compassion, mercy and tenderness of God.

Your Soul on the Spiritual Path

The lower figure in the Chart of Your Divine Self represents you on the spiritual path. This is how you would look had you been invoking the violet flame for some time. The violet flame is the action of the Holy Spirit, the Third Person of the Trinity.

The lower figure also shows you wearing a robe of white, as do the saints in heaven.[8] Your threefold flame is balanced and sealed in the secret chamber of the heart. Your halo reveals a state of holiness, right mindfulness and your emergent sainthood.

Surrounding the violet flame is your tube of light, a cylinder of white light that descends from your I AM Presence, in answer to your call, to protect you from harmful energies. Students of the ascended masters invoke the tube of light in the morning and at intervals throughout the day, especially when the negative energies of the planet are at their peak.

Your tube of light will protect you twenty-four hours a day as long as you remain harmonious. In times of stress, you may also find it necessary to call to Archangel Michael to protect you, your loved ones and all souls of light worldwide.

The soul is the living potential of God—the part of yourself that is mortal but that can become immortal. The purpose of your soul's evolution on earth is to perfect herself under the tutelage of your Holy Christ Self, your I AM Presence and the ascended masters so that she can return to God.

Paul envisioned the soul's final victory over all that would oppose her ascent back to God when he proclaimed: "This corruptible must put on incorruption, and this mortal *must* put on immortality. So when this corruptible shall have put on incorruption, and this mortal shall have put on immortality, then shall be brought to pass the saying that is written, Death is swallowed up in victory."[9]

The soul becomes immortal when after lifetimes of service to God and humanity she reunites with her I AM Presence in the ritual of the ascension, as Jesus and other ascended masters have done. The ascension is the goal of life for every soul. The soul may go through numerous incarnations before she perfects herself on the path of personal Christhood and is thereby worthy to make her ascension.

What happens to the soul between incarnations? When the soul concludes a lifetime on earth, the I AM Presence withdraws the crystal cord, the threefold flame returns to the heart of the Holy Christ Self and the soul gravitates to the highest level of consciousness to which she has attained in her incarnations.

If the soul merits it, between incarnations she is schooled in the retreats of the ascended masters in the heaven-world. There she studies under the archangels and masters of wisdom to prepare for her next incarnation.

If lifetime after lifetime the soul does not exercise her free will to glorify God—and to be bonded to her Holy Christ Self in the process—her opportunity to become immortal will ultimately come to an end. The soul may cease to retain her soul blueprint and her self-identification in God. This is what is meant by the "second death."[10]

To achieve the goal of immortality and ascend, the soul must first become one with her Holy Christ Self, balance at least 51 percent of her karma and fulfill her mission on earth. As Saint Germain explains it, balancing 51 percent of your karma means that you have transmuted and put to constructive use 51 percent of the energy God has ever given to you.

When your soul at last takes flight and ascends back to God, you will become an ascended master and be free from the round of karma and rebirth. And you will receive the crown of everlasting life.

The Violet Flame
for Physical and Spiritual
Transformation

Call upon the violet transmuting flame to surround
the four lower bodies. This will invariably spiritualize
consciousness if the supplicant truly
desires to be one with God.

LANTO

Just as a ray of sunlight passing through a prism is refracted into the seven colors of the rainbow, so spiritual light manifests as seven rays. The violet ray is the seventh of these rays. Each ray has a specific color, frequency and quality (see page 175). When you invoke a ray in the name of God, it manifests as a "flame." You could compare this to a ray of sunlight that passes through a magnifying glass and creates a flame.

Each of the spiritual flames creates a specific positive action in the body, heart, mind and soul. The violet flame creates an action of mercy, justice, freedom and transmutation.

To transmute is to alter in form, appearance or nature, especially to change something into a higher form. The term was used by alchemists who attempted to transmute base metals into gold, separating the "subtle" from the "gross" by means of heat. For both ancient and medieval alchemists, the real purpose of alchemical transmutation was spiritual transformation and the attainment of eternal life.

That is precisely what the violet flame can do for us. It consumes the elements of our karma, separating them from our native purity, so that we can realize the true gold of our Higher Self and achieve a lasting spiritual transformation.

In our physical world, violet light has the shortest wavelength and therefore the highest frequency in the visible spectrum. Thus, in one sense of the word, the violet light can be seen as a point of transition from the visible to the invisible, from one plane of being to the next.

Since frequency is directly proportional to energy, and violet light has the highest frequency in the visible spectrum, the violet light also has the most energy. That means that it also has the greatest ability to change matter at the atomic level.

Correspondingly, Saint Germain says that "the violet flame is the supreme antidote for physical problems." He explains that the violet flame has the ability to change physical conditions because, of all the rays, the violet is closest in vibratory action to the components of matter. "The violet flame can combine with any molecule or molecular structure, any particle of matter known or unknown, and any wave of light, electron or electricity," he says. Wherever people gather together to give violet-flame decrees, "there you notice immediately an improvement in physical conditions."[1]

What Can the Violet Flame Do for You?

The violet flame can literally consume the debris within and between the atoms of your being. It is like soaking them in a chemical solution that, layer by layer, dissolves the dirt that has been trapped there for thousands of years.

With regular use, the violet flame can create positive change at all levels of your being. It can increase your stamina. It can help you overcome blocks to healing physical problems or emotional hang-ups. It is the joie de vivre that can lift your spirits. And it can transmute the buildup of mankind's karma that could result in the darkness prophesied for our time. That is exactly why Saint Germain, out of his great compassion for our souls, gave us the colossal gift of the violet flame in this century.

If you would like to experiment with the violet flame, you can recite the following affirmations and prayers.

I AM the Violet Flame

Visualization:

"I AM the Violet Flame" is a powerful affirmation. It is short and you can repeat it many times to build a strong momentum of violet flame.

Visualize yourself surrounded by the violet flame as you see it in the Chart of Your Divine Self around the lower figure. See the violet flame come to life as if you were looking at a movie. The flames rise and pulsate around you in different shades and gradations of purple, pink and violet. See these flames pass through your body, caressing each organ and restoring wholeness. See them saturating your mind and your emotions, relieving all burdens.

You can also visualize the seven seas filled with violet flame. Meditate on the power of the seven seas and then translate that thoughtform to a giant, peaceful violet-flame sea that envelops the entire planet. Imagine the weight of it, the power of it, the energy of it! The violet flame has the capacity to totally transform the planetary body.

You can use this decree for specific situations. For instance, you can see the violet-flame sea transmuting pollution in the seas of the world. Or you can focus on the world's children. Visualize them before you, starting with the children of your own neighborhood and moving on to the needy children of the world. See frolicking, dancing violet flames swaddling them and transforming their burdens into joy.

Decree:

> I AM the violet flame
>   In action in me now
> I AM the violet flame
>   To Light alone I bow
> I AM the violet flame
>   In mighty cosmic power
> I AM the light of God
>   Shining every hour
> I AM the violet flame
>   Blazing like a sun
> I AM God's sacred power
>   Freeing every one

More Violet Fire

Visualization:

The mantra "More Violet Fire" is known for its rhythm and for the spiraling action of the violet flame that follows the rhythm. As you recite this mantra, commune with your I AM Presence. Feel the love of your Presence enfold you completely as you let go of all anger, worries, concerns and fears.

Visualize a waterfall of light descending from your I AM Presence. See this light being released through your chakras as streams of glistening energy going forth to bless and comfort those for whom you are praying. See the violet flame dissolving the cause, effect, record and memory of your own and others' misdeeds.

As you say these words, you can also visualize your own special images of what you want the violet flame to accomplish. No problem is too insignificant or too big to tackle with the violet flame.

Mantra:

Lovely God Presence, I AM in me,
Hear me now I do decree:
Bring to pass each blessing for which I call
Upon the Holy Christ Self of each and all.

Let violet fire of freedom roll
Round the world to make all whole.
Saturate the earth and its people, too,
With increasing Christ-radiance shining through!

I AM this action from God above,
Sustained by the hand of heaven's love,
Transmuting the causes of discord here,
Removing the cores so that none do fear.

I AM, I AM, I AM
The full power of freedom's love,
Raising all earth to heaven above.
Violet fire now blazing bright,
In living beauty is God's own light

Which right now and forever
Sets the world, myself and all life
Eternally free in ascended master perfection!
Almighty I AM! Almighty I AM! Almighty I AM!

To learn more about the violet flame, see *Violet Flame to Heal Body, Mind and Soul* by Elizabeth Clare Prophet, Summit University Press.

Notes

Chapter 1

Opening quotation: Jesus, *The Book of Thomas the Contender,* in James M. Robinson, ed., *The Nag Hammadi Library in English,* 3d ed., rev. (San Francisco: Harper and Row, 1988), p. 201.

1. Matt. 5:16.
2. Matt. 5:14.
3. Matt. 7:12.
4. Matt. 21:12.
5. Eph. 4:26.
6. What can you do if you can't resolve an inharmonious situation in a given day but are determined not to allow your *ka* to act out your anger while you sleep at night? You can call to Archangel Michael to seal your anger, to box it up.

   Visualize a strong box wrapped in shiny blue metallic paper and tied with a blue ribbon. See all of the unresolved feelings and issues in your life sealed in that blue box. You can visualize the blue box around your subconscious and unconscious as well. Then call for the Holy Spirit as the violet flame to consume your anger and to saturate the contents of the box with God's purifying fire.

Chapter 2

Opening quotation: Marsilio Ficino, in Paul Oskar Kristeller, *The Philosophy of Marcilio Ficino,* trans. Virginia Conant (New York: Columbia University Press, 1943).

1. Meister Eckhart, quoted in Sidney Spencer, *Mysticism in World Religion* (1963; reprint, Gloucester, Mass.: Peter Smith, 1971), p. 245.

2. *Meister Eckhart: Sermons and Treatises,* trans. M. O'C. Walshe (Longmead, Shaftesbury, Dorset: Element Books, 1987), 3:107.

3. Ibid.

4. Heb. 12:29.

5. James 4:8.

6. Samuel Taylor Coleridge, *Biographia Literaria,* chap. 14.

7. Shakespeare, *King Lear,* act 5, sc. 3, line 176.

8. Matt. 13:24–30.

9. The flames of God are many. The most important flames for our use correspond to the seven rays (see glossary). A simple method of visualizing the flames

is to fix in your mind the memory of a blazing campfire. See the physical flames take on the color of the God-flame you desire to invoke. Now enlarge your image of the flames to fill your entire consciousness. Then visualize yourself stepping into the center of God's flaming Presence and feel his love enfold you as a thousand-petaled lotus—each flame a petal of God's all-embracing consciousness. *The Creative Power of Sound,* published by Summit University Press, will help you to sustain your visualization of the flames of God as you give mantras, decrees and affirmations.

10. I Cor. 15:37–41.
11. Acts 2:1–4; Matt. 3:11.
12. I Cor. 15:42–45.
13. Prov. 3:5.
14. Heb. 11:1.

Chapter 3

Opening quotation: The Zohar 1:78a, quoted in Daniel Matt, *The Essential Kabbalah* (HarperSanFrancisco, 1996), p. 127.

1. "Overheard in an Orchard" by Elizabeth Cheney.
2. Matt. 10:39.
3. Exod. 20:3.
4. Exod. 20:5, 6.
5. Matt. 6:1–4.

6. Matt. 13:29.
7. Matt. 11:12.
8. II Tim. 2:15.
9. Matt. 25:21.
10. Deut. 6:4.
11. Matt. 2:2.
12. Luke 12:32.
13. I John 3:2.

Chapter 4

Opening quotation: Sri Ramana Maharshi, quoted in Andrew Harvey and Anne Baring, comps., *The Mystic Vision: Daily Encounters with the Divine* (Harper-SanFrancisco, 1995), p. 26.

1. Ps. 8:4–9.
2. Exod. 20:3.
3. Gal. 6:7.
4. Acts 9:5.
5. I Cor. 8:5.
6. Prov. 16:32
7. Eccles. 1:14, 15.
8. John 14:12.
9. James 2:19.
10. Ps. 8:5.
11. Matt. 10:39.
12. Eph. 5:26.
13. Col. 3:9, 10.

14. I Cor. 15:26.
15. "Know thyself" is an ancient proverb attributed to several sources, among them Thales and Solon of Athens (two of the Seven Wise Men of Greece) and Socrates. Cicero speaks of it as a precept of Apollo. It was one of the maxims inscribed in gold letters over the portico of the temple at Delphi.

Chapter 5

Opening quotation: Kabir, in Rabindranath Tagore, trans., *Songs of Kabir* (York Beach, Me.: Samuel Weiser, 1991), p. 47.

1. Ps. 1:2.
2. I Thess. 5:19.
3. Matt. 11:12.
4. Matt. 6:33.

Chapter 6

Opening quotation: Lao Tzu, in Brian Walker, trans., *Hua Hu Ching: Teachings of Lao Tzu* (Livingston, Mont.: Clark City Press, 1992), p. 96.

1. Matt. 25:14–30.
2. Matt. 10:28.
3. James 1:17.
4. Gal. 6:7.
5. Luke 15:11–32.
6. Matt. 25:29.
7. The place where God is: "Our God is a consuming

fire" (Heb. 12:29).

8. See Elizabeth Clare Prophet, *Violet Flame to Heal Body, Mind and Soul* (Corwin Springs, Mont.: Summit University Press, 1997).

9. Mark 10:13–16.

10. Gen. 1:26, 28.

Chapter 7

1. Gen. 1:26.

2. John 10:7, 9.

3. I Cor. 15:50.

4. I Cor. 15:31.

5. Mark 1:11.

Chapter 8

Opening quotation: Mother Teresa, in Teresa de Bertodano, ed., *Daily Readings with Mother Teresa* (London: Fount Paperbacks, HarperCollinsPublishers, 1993), p. 117.

1. The author recommends the reading of *The Screwtape Letters* by C. S. Lewis (New York: Macmillan Publishing Co., 1961) in connection with the series on *Understanding Yourself.*

2. Luke 11:52.

3. Matt. 7:9.

4. Acts 20:35.

5. Luke 1:52.

Chapter 9

Opening quotation: Gautama Buddha, in H. Saddha-tissa, trans., *The Sutta-Nipata* (London: Curzon Press, 1985), p. 96.

1. Matt. 19:30.
2. I Thess. 2:19.
3. Ps. 1:4.
4. Matt. 10:37.
5. Gen. 16; 17:15–21; Gal. 4:22–23. The Son of promise is Abraham's son Isaac, who is symbolic of the Real Self appearing as the fusion of the light of the Father-Mother God within us.
6. John 3:1–21.
7. I Cor. 15:47–49.

Chapter 10

Opening quotation: I Kings 3: 7, 9.

1. Gen. 4:1–16.
2. Rev. 3:11.
3. John 5:39.

Chapter 11

Opening quotation: Teresa of Avila, from a bookmark in her Breviary.

1. Matt. 5:5.
2. Prov. 4:7.
3. Matt. 16:23.
4. II Tim. 2:15.

Chapter 12

Opening quotation: Rumi, in Coleman Barks et al., trans., *The Essential Rumi* (HarperSanFrancisco, 1995), pp. 223–24.

1. Acts 17:26.
2. Ps. 2:1.
3. Paul Carus, comp., *The Gospel of Buddha,* quoted in *The World's Great Scriptures,* comp. Lewis Browne (New York: Macmillan Publishing Co., 1961), p. 173.
4. Ibid., p. 172.
5. Rudyard Kipling, "If," stanzas 1, 4.

Chapter 13

Opening quotation: Chandogya Upanishad 8:1, in Juan Mascaró, trans., *The Upanishads* (Baltimore, Md.: Penguin Books, 1965), p. 120.

1. Gen. 1:26, 31.
2. Gal. 6:7, 8.
3. John 1:9.
4. I Pet. 3:4.
5. Rev. 1:18.
6. Mark 10:31.
7. John 3:7.

Chapter 14

1. John 1:1.
2. Matt. 3:12.

3. Prov. 14:12.
4. Gen. 2:7; 3:19.
5. Gen. 1:26.
6. I John 3:2.
7. I Cor. 3:19.
8. Acts 9:5.
9. II Cor. 9:7.

Chapter 15

Opening quotation: Marcus Aurelius, from *Meditations.*

1. Isa. 53:5.
2. Heb. 10:17.
3. Heb. 7:25.
4. Ps. 1:2.
5. John 14:2.
6. I Cor. 10:4.

Chapter 16

Opening quotation: Henry Wadsworth Longfellow, from "The Poets."

1. I Cor. 6:19, 20.
2. Eph. 2:19–21.
3. John 10:1.
4. John 8:12.
5. Matt. 18:3, 4.

Your Divine Self

Opening quotation: Symeon the New Theologian, quoted in Andrew Harvey, ed., *The Essential Mystics: Selections from the World's Great Wisdom Traditions* (HarperSanFrancisco, 1996), p. 190.

1. James 4:8.
2. Matt. 6:20, 21.
3. Deut. 6:4.
4. Col. 2:9.
5. Eccles. 12:6.
6. *Ratnagotravibhāga* 1.28, in Edward Conze et al., eds., *Buddhist Texts through the Ages* (1954; reprint, New York: Harper and Row, Harper Torchbooks, 1964), p. 181.
7. *The Upanishads,* trans. Juan Mascaró (1974; reprint, Baltimore: Penguin Books, 1965), pp. 61, 60, 59.
8. Rev. 3:4, 5; 6:9–11; 7:9, 13–17; 19:7, 8, 14.
9. I Cor. 15:53, 54.
10. Rev. 2:11; 20:6, 11–15; 21:8.

The Violet Flame for
Physical and Spiritual Transformation

Opening quotation: Lanto, "Human Moods," in *Understanding Yourself,* p. 119 of this book.

1. Saint Germain, December 2, 1984, in *Maitreya On the Image of God,* Book II (1984 *Pearls of Wisdom,* vol. 27) (Corwin Springs, Mont.: Summit University Press, 1990), p. 553.

Glossary

Words set in italics are defined elsewhere in the glossary.

Akashic records. The impressions of all that has ever transpired in the physical universe, recorded in an etheric substance and dimension known as akasha. These records can be read by those with developed soul faculties.

Archangel Michael. The Angel of the LORD who stands in defense of the Christ consciousness in all children of God; also known as Prince of the Archangels and Defender of the Faith. He is the most revered angel in Jewish, Christian and Islamic scripture and tradition.

Ascended masters. Enlightened spiritual beings who once lived on earth, fulfilled their reason for being and have ascended, or reunited with God. The ascended masters are the true teachers of mankind. They direct the spiritual evolution of all devotees of God and guide them back to their source.

Ascension. A spiritual acceleration of consciousness that takes place at the natural conclusion of one's final lifetime on earth whereby the soul reunites with God and is free from the round of *karma* and rebirth. *See also* p. 181.

Astral plane. The lowest vibrating frequency of time and space; the repository of mankind's thoughts and feelings, conscious and unconscious.

Avatar. From Sanskrit *avatara,* literally "descent." A Hindu term for an incarnation of God on earth.

Bodhisattva. A being of bodhi, or enlightenment, who has foregone the bliss of Nirvana (the highest transcendent consciousness in Buddhism) with a vow to save every being on earth.

Brotherhood. *See* Great White Brotherhood.

Brothers of the Golden Robe. A spiritual order of ascended and unascended beings sponsored by the *Great White Brotherhood* who are dedicated to the illumination of mankind.

Causal Body. Interpenetrating spheres of light surrounding each one's *I AM Presence* at spiritual levels. The spheres of the Causal Body contain the records of the virtuous acts we have performed to the glory of God and the blessing of man through our many incarnations on earth. *See also* pp. 174–75.

Chakra. Sanskrit, meaning "wheel," "disc" or "circle." Term used to denote the centers of *light* anchored in the etheric body and governing the flow of energy to the *four lower bodies* of man.

Christ. From the Greek *Christos,* meaning "anointed." One fully endued and infilled, i.e., anointed, with the light of God; the *Word,* the Logos, the Mediator, the Second Person of the Trinity. In the Hindu Trinity of Brahma, Vishnu and Shiva, the term *Christ* corresponds to or is the incarnation of Vishnu, the Preserver.

Christ Self. Our inner teacher, guardian, friend and advocate before God; the *Universal Christ* individualized for each of us. The true identity of the *soul;* the *Real Self* of every man, woman and child to which the soul must rise. When one achieves the fullness of soul-identification with the Christ Self, he achieves *Christ* consciousness and is called a Christed, or anointed, one.

Darjeeling Council. A council of the *Great White Brotherhood* consisting of *ascended masters* and unascended disciples headquartered at an etheric *retreat* over Darjeeling, India. Its main objective is to train *souls* for world service in God-government and the economy.

Decree. A dynamic form of spoken prayer used by students of the *ascended masters* to direct God's *light* into individual and world conditions.

Divine Manchild. The incarnation of the *Universal Christ* for the Aquarian age in the one and the many sons and daughters of God whose destiny it is to focus the *Christ* consciousness to the evolutions of earth.

Divine Mother. The feminine polarity of the Godhead, the manifestation of God as Mother. Matter is the feminine polarity of *Spirit,* and the term is used interchangeably with Mater, Latin meaning "mother." In this context, the entire material world becomes the womb of creation into which Spirit projects the energies of life.

Divine Presence. *See* I AM Presence.

Divine Self. *See* Higher Self.

Divine spark. *See* Threefold flame.

Elementals. Beings of earth, air, fire and water; nature spirits who are the servants of God and man. The elementals establish and maintain the physical platform for the *soul's* evolution. The elementals who serve the fire element are called salamanders; those who serve the air element, sylphs; those who serve the water element, undines; and those who serve the earth element, gnomes.

Fallen angels. The angels who followed Lucifer in the Great Rebellion and whose consciousness therefore "fell" to lower levels of vibration and awareness as they were "cast out into the earth" at the hand of Archangel Michael. By the karma of their disobedience to God and his *Christ* and their blasphemy of his children, they were constrained to take on and evolve through dense physical bodies.

Father-Mother God. The divine wholeness spoken of by

the Lord *Christ* as "the beginning and the ending," Alpha and Omega, in Revelation. Through the *Universal Christ,* the *Word* incarnate, the Father is the origin and the Mother is the fulfillment of the cycles of God's consciousness expressed throughout the Spirit-Matter creation.

Fiat. An authoritative decision; a command, order or pronouncement; a short dynamic invocation or decree usually using the name of God, I AM, such as: "I AM the Way!" "I AM the Truth!"or "I AM the Resurrection and the Life!"

Four lower bodies. The vehicles the soul uses in her journey on earth; the four sheaths surrounding the soul: (1) the etheric, or memory, body; (2) the mental body; (3) the desire, or emotional, body; (4) the physical body.

The three higher bodies of the soul are the *Christ Self,* the *I AM Presence* and the *Causal Body.*

God-flame. The *sacred fire;* the identity, being, and consciousness of God in and as the white fire core of being. See also Threefold flame.

God Presence. *See* I AM Presence.

Great Central Sun. The center of cosmos; the point of integration of the Spirit-Matter cosmos; the point of origin of all physical-spiritual creation; also called the Great Hub.

Greater Self. *See* Higher Self.

Great White Brotherhood. A spiritual fraternity of *ascended masters,* archangels and other advanced spiritual beings. The term "white" refers not to race but to the aura of white *light* that surrounds these immortals. The Great White Brotherhood works with earnest seekers of every race, religion and walk of life to assist humanity. The Brotherhood also includes certain unascended disciples of the ascended masters.

Higher Self. The *I AM Presence;* the *Christ Self;* the exalted aspect of selfhood. Used in contrast to *lower self,* or little self, which indicates that which is in a state of becoming whole and attaining the realization of self as God.

Holy Christ Self. *See* Christ Self.

Holy Spirit. Third Person of the Trinity; the cloven tongues of fire which focus the *Father-Mother God;* also called the *sacred fire.* In the Hindu Trinity of Brahma, Vishnu and Shiva, the Holy Spirit corresponds to Shiva.

I AM Presence. The Presence of God, the I AM THAT I AM, individualized for each of us. *See also* p. 174.

Jesus Christ. The *ascended master;* the *avatar* of the Piscean age; the incarnation of the *Word,* the *Universal Christ.* Jesus came to reveal the individual *Christ Self* to all mankind and to show the works of the Father (the *I AM Presence*) that can be accomplished by his sons and daughters.

Karma. Sanskrit, meaning action, work or deed. The consequences of one's thoughts, words and deeds of this life and previous lives; the law of cause and effect, which decrees that whatever we do, for good or for ill, comes full circle to our doorstep.

Karmic Board. *See* Lords of Karma.

Lifestream. The stream of life that comes forth from the *Spirit* and descends to the planes of matter where it manifests as the *threefold flame* anchored in the *secret chamber of the heart.* Used to denote the ongoing nature of the soul through its cycles of individualization.

Light. The universal radiance and energy of God.

Lords of Karma. The ascended beings who comprise the Karmic Board. The Lords of Karma dispense justice to this system of worlds, adjudicating *karma,* mercy and judgment on behalf of every *lifestream.* All *souls* must pass before the Karmic Board before and after each incarnation on earth, receiving their assignment and karmic allotment for each lifetime beforehand and the review of their performance at its conclusion.

Little self. *See* Lower self.

Lower self. The lesser self, or human self, as opposed to the *Higher Self;* identity based on limitation and the laws of mortality.

Luciferian. Of or relating to Lucifer, the archangel who fell from grace through pride and ambition. The angels who followed Lucifer are called Luciferians, Satanists or sons of Belial.

Macrocosm. Greek, meaning "great world." The larger cosmos; the entire warp and woof of creation. Also used to contrast man as the *microcosm,* "the little world," against the backdrop of the larger world in which he lives.

Maha Chohan. The representative of the *Holy Spirit* to earth and her evolutions; also known as the Great Lord of the *seven rays.*

Mantra. A mystical word or formula, often in Sanskrit, to be recited or sung for the purpose of intensifying the action of the spirit of God in man.

Manu. Sanskrit for the progenitor and lawgiver of the evolutions of God on earth. The Manu and his divine complement are assigned by the *Father-Mother God* to sponsor and ensoul the Christic image for a certain evolution of souls known as a "root race."

Microcosm. From the Greek, meaning "small world." (1) The world of the individual—his *four lower bodies,* his aura and the forcefield of his *karma.* (2) The planet. *See also* Macrocosm.

Monad. The human monad is the entire forcefield of self that makes up the self-awareness which identifies itself as human. It is composed of interconnecting spheres of influences—hereditary, environmental and karmic. The divine monad consists of the *I AM*

Presence and *Causal Body* of the individual.

Mother of Mercy. The ascended lady master Kuan Yin. She is known as the Mother of Mercy, or Goddess of Mercy, because she ensouls the God-qualities of mercy, compassion and forgiveness. Kuan Yin ascended thousands of years ago and has taken the vow of the *Bodhisattva* to serve planet earth until all her evolutions are free.

Mystery school. A retreat maintained by the *Great White Brotherhood* which serves as a repository for the knowledge of the sacred mysteries that is vouchsafed to souls when they have demonstrated the necessary discipline and love.

Octaves of light. Realms or planes of perfection beyond the earthly realms of time and space.

Path. The strait and narrow way that leadeth unto life. (Matt. 7:14) The spiritual path whereby the disciple who pursues the *Christ* consciousness overcomes step by step the limitations of selfhood and attains reunion with God through the ritual of the *ascension.*

Presence. *See* I AM Presence.

Real Self. *See* Higher Self.

Retreat. The spiritual home of an *ascended master* or heavenly being. Retreats are located chiefly in the heaven-world.

Sacred fire. God, *light,* life, energy, the I AM THAT I AM. "Our God is a consuming fire." (Heb. 12:29) The

Kundalini fire that lies as the coiled serpent in the base-of-the-spine *chakra* and rises through spiritual purity and self-mastery to the crown chakra, quickening the other spiritual centers along the way.

Saint Germain. The *ascended master* who is hierarch of the Aquarian age and sponsor of the United States of America. He ensouls the God-qualities of freedom, mercy and forgiveness. He teaches us to invoke the *violet flame* to transmute our *karma* and win our immortal freedom.

Satanism. The practices of those who follow Satan. Satan was a lieutenant of Lucifer, the fallen archangel, and a ranking member of his false hierarchy.

Secret chamber of the heart. A central spiritual chamber behind the heart chakra surrounded by great *light* and protection. It is the connecting point of the cord of light that descends from your *I AM Presence* to sustain the beating of your physical heart, giving you life, purpose and cosmic integration. It is the special place where you commune with your *Christ Self* and fan the fires of your *threefold flame*.

Seven rays. The *light* emanations of the Godhead. The seven rays of the white light which emerge through the prism of the *Christ* consciousness. Each ray focuses a frequency, or color, and specific qualities: (1) blue—faith, will, power, perfection and protection; (2) yellow—wisdom, understanding, enlightenment, and illumination; (3) pink—compassion, kindness, charity, love and beauty; (4) white—purity, discipline, order and joy; (5) green—truth, science, healing, music, abundance and vision; (6) purple and gold—ministration, service, peace and brotherhood; (7) violet—freedom, mercy, justice, transmutation and forgiveness.

Son of God. The Second Person of the Trinity; the individualization of the *Universal Christ;* the *Real Self* of each person. *See also* Christ Self.

Soul. God is *Spirit* and the soul is the living potential of God. The purpose of the soul's evolution on earth is to perfect herself under the tutelage of her *Holy Christ Self, I AM Presence* and the *ascended masters* so that she can return to God.

Spirit. The masculine polarity of the Godhead; the coordinate of matter; God as Father, or Brahma; the plane of the *I AM Presence,* of perfection. (When lowercased, as in "spirit," the term is used interchangeably with *soul.*)

The Summit Lighthouse. An outer organization of the *Great White Brotherhood* founded by Mark L. Prophet in 1958 under the direction of the *ascended master* El Morya to publish the teachings of the ascended masters.

Threefold flame. The flame of God ensconced within the *secret chamber of the heart;* the soul's point of contact with her source; the divine spark; the heart flame. It is composed of three intertwining flames: the blue flame of power, the yellow flame of wisdom and the pink flame of love. These three flames also correspond to the Trinity: Father (Brahma), Son (Vishnu) and Holy Spirit (Shiva). *See also* pp. 178–80.

True Self. *See* Higher Self.

Twin flame. The *soul's* masculine or feminine counterpart conceived out of the same white fire body, the fiery ovoid of the *I AM Presence.*

Unfed flame. *See* Threefold flame.

Universal Christ. The mediator between the planes of *Spirit* and the planes of matter; personified as the *Christ Self,* he is the mediator between the Spirit of God and the *soul* of man.

Violet flame. The *sacred fire* of the Holy Spirit that transmutes the cause, effect, record and memory of sin, or negative *karma.* Also called the flame of transmutation, of freedom and of forgiveness. *See also* pp. 183–89.

Word. The Logos; the power of God and the realization of that power incarnate in and as the *Christ.* It is through the Word that the *Father-Mother God* communicates with mankind.

KUTHUMI, LANTO and MERU are sages dedicated to helping us realize our full potential through the education of the heart, mind and soul. Schooled in both Eastern and Western spiritual traditions, they bring a unique approach to the mastery of the self and its components in both subconscious and superconscious levels of awareness.

Kuthumi, Lanto and Meru have worked with Mark L. Prophet and Elizabeth Clare Prophet to publish their teachings on how to walk the path of compassionate enlightenment—a path that cultivates profound spirituality not only for personal growth but also for the nurturing of those in need.

Mark and Elizabeth Prophet are pioneers of modern spirituality. They have conducted seminars and workshops throughout the world on practical spirituality and the mystical paths of the world's religions. They have also published a number of books on these topics, including *The Human Aura, The Lost Years of Jesus, Kabbalah: Key to Your Inner Power* and *Reincarnation: The Missing Link in Christianity.* Mark passed on in 1973, and Elizabeth carries on their work from her home in Montana.

Other titles from
Summit University Press

Reincarnation: The Missing Link in Christianity
The Lost Years of Jesus
The Lost Teachings of Jesus
Quietly Comes the Buddha
Kabbalah: Key to Your Inner Power
The Human Aura
Saint Germain On Alchemy
Forbidden Mysteries of Enoch
The Answer You're Looking For Is Inside of You
How to Work with Angels
The Creative Power of Sound
Access the Power of Your Higher Self
Violet Flame to Heal Body, Mind and Soul
Creative Abundance
Nurturing Your Baby's Soul

Summit University Press titles are available from fine bookstores everywhere, including Barnes and Noble, B. Dalton Bookseller, Borders, Hastings and Waldenbooks.

To request a free catalog of books and tapes or for information about seminars and conferences with Elizabeth Clare Prophet, write to PO Box 5000, Corwin Springs, Montana 59030-5000 USA, or call 1-888-700-8087. Fax 1-800-221-8307 (406-848-9555 outside the U.S.A.) E-mail us at tslinfo@tsl.org   Visit our web site at www.tsl.org